Evaluation of the Voluntary National Tests

PHASE 1

Lauress L. Wise, Robert M. Hauser, Karen J. Mitchell, and Michael J. Feuer

Board on Testing and Assessment

Commission on Behavioral and Social Sciences and Education

National Research Council

NATIONAL ACADEMY PRESS
Washington, D.C. 1999

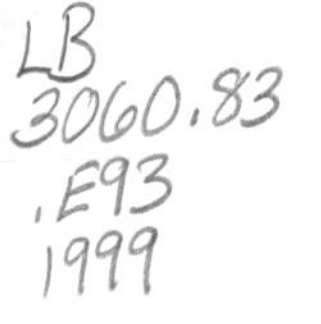

NATIONAL ACADEMY PRESS • 2101 Constitution Avenue, N.W. • Washington, D.C. 20418

NOTICE: The project that is the subject of this report was approved by the Governing Board of the National Research Council, whose members are drawn from the councils of the National Academy of Sciences, the National Academy of Engineering, and the Institute of Medicine. The co-principal investigators responsible for the report were chosen for their special competence.

The National Academy of Sciences is a private, nonprofit, self-perpetuating society of distinguished scholars engaged in scientific and engineering research, dedicated to the furtherance of science and technology and to their use for the general welfare. Upon the authority of the charter granted to it by the Congress in 1863, the Academy has a mandate that requires it to advise the federal government on scientific and technical matters. Dr. Bruce M. Alberts is president of the National Academy of Sciences.

The National Academy of Engineering was established in 1964, under the charter of the National Academy of Sciences, as a parallel organization of outstanding engineers. It is autonomous in its administration and in the selection of its members, sharing with the National Academy of Sciences the responsibility for advising the federal government. The National Academy of Engineering also sponsors engineering programs aimed at meeting national needs, encourages education and research, and recognizes the superior achievements of engineers. Dr. William A. Wulf is president of the National Academy of Engineering.

The Institute of Medicine was established in 1970 by the National Academy of Sciences to secure the services of eminent members of appropriate professions in the examination of policy matters pertaining to the health of the public. The Institute acts under the responsibility given to the National Academy of Sciences by its congressional charter to be an adviser to the federal government and, upon its own initiative, to identify issues of medical care, research, and education. Dr. Kenneth I. Shine is president of the Institute of Medicine.

The National Research Council was organized by the National Academy of Sciences in 1916 to associate the broad community of science and technology with the Academy's purposes of furthering knowledge and advising the federal government. Functioning in accordance with general policies determined by the Academy, the Council has become the principal operating agency of both the National Academy of Sciences and the National Academy of Engineering in providing services to the government, the public, and the scientific and engineering communities. The Council is administered jointly by both Academies and the Institute of Medicine. Dr. Bruce M. Alberts and Dr. William A. Wulf are chairman and vice chairman, respectively, of the National Research Council.

The study was supported by Contract/Grant No. RJ97184001 between the National Academy of Sciences and the U.S. Department of Education. Any opinions, findings, conclusions, or recommendations expressed in this publication are those of the author(s) and do not necessarily reflect the view of the organizations or agencies that provided support for this project.

International Standard Book Number 0-309-06277-2

Additional copies of this report are available from:
National Academy Press
2101 Constitution Avenue N.W.
Washington, D.C. 20418
Call 800-624-6242 or 202-334-3313 (in the Washington Metropolitan Area).

This report is also available on line at **http://www.nap.edu**

Printed in the United States of America

PROJECT ON THE EVALUATION OF THE VOLUNTARY NATIONAL TESTS

Co-Principal Investigators

ROBERT M. HAUSER, University of Wisconsin, Madison

LAURESS L. WISE, Human Resources Research Organization, Alexandria, Virginia

Staff, Board on Testing and Assessment

MICHAEL J. FEUER, *Director*

KAREN J. MITCHELL, *Senior Program Officer*

STEPHEN E. BALDWIN, *Senior Program Officer*

MARILYN DABADY, *Research Associate*

VIOLA C. HOREK, *Administrative Associate*

DOROTHY R. MAJEWSKI, *Senior Project Assistant*

Foreword

President Clinton's 1997 proposal to create voluntary national tests in reading and mathematics catapulted testing to the top of the national education agenda. The proposal turned up the volume on what had already been a contentious debate and drew intense scrutiny from a wide range of educators, parents, policy makers, and social scientists. Recognizing the important role science could play in sorting through the passionate and often heated exchanges in the testing debate, Congress and the Clinton administration asked the National Research Council, through its Board on Testing and Assessment (BOTA), to conduct three fast-track studies over a 10-month period.

This report and its companions—*Uncommon Measures: Equivalence and Linkage Among Educational Tests* and *High Stakes: Testing for Tracking, Promotion, and Graduation*—are the result of truly heroic efforts on the part of the BOTA members, the study committee chairs and members, two co-principal investigators, consultants, and staff, who all understood the urgency of the mission and rose to the challenge of a unique and daunting timeline. Michael Feuer, BOTA director, deserves the special thanks of the Board for keeping the effort on track and shepherding the report through the review process. His dedicated effort, long hours, sage advice, and good humor were essential to the success of this effort. Robert Hauser and Lauress Wise deserve our deepest appreciation for their outstanding commitment of time, energy, and intellectual firepower that made this evaluation possible.

These reports are exemplars of the Research Council's commitment to scientific rigor in the public interest: they provide clear and compelling statements of the underlying issues, cogent answers to nettling questions, and highly readable findings and recommendations. These reports will help illuminate the toughest issues in the ongoing debate over the proposed Voluntary National Tests. But they will do much more as well. The issues addressed in this and the other two reports go well beyond the immediate national testing proposal: they have much to contribute to knowledge about the way tests—all tests—are planned, designed, implemented, reported, and used for a variety of education policy goals.

I know the whole board joins me in expressing our deepest gratitude to the many people who worked so hard on this project. These reports will advance the debate over the role of testing in American education, and I am honored to have participated in this effort.

Robert L. Linn, *Chair*
Board on Testing and Assessment

Acknowledgments

This project would not have been possible without the generosity of many individuals and the contributions of several institutions.

The sage counsel of Bob Linn and Carl Kaestle, chair and vice chair of the Board on Testing and Assessment (BOTA), helped us frame the evaluation and test our findings and conclusions. Other BOTA members contributed in important ways by participating in briefings and making invaluable suggestions for improved analysis and discussion.

The Office of Planning and Evaluation Services, U.S. Department of Education, administered the contract for this evaluation. Director Allen Ginsburg provided assistance in planning the evaluation, and Audrey Pendleton served as an exemplary contracting officer's technical representative during this first phase of the evaluation. We thank them for their guidance and support.

Staff from the National Assessment Governing Board (NAGB), under the leadership of Roy Truby, executive director, and the NAGB prime contractor, the American Institutes for Research (AIR), with Archie LaPointe's guidance, were a valuable source of information and data on the design and development of the Voluntary National Tests (VNT). Sharif Shakrani, Raymond Fields, and Mary Crovo of NAGB and Mark Kutner, Steven Ferrara, John Olsen, Clayton Best, Roger Levine, Terry Salinger, Fran Stancavage, and Christine Paulson of AIR provided us with important information on occasions that are too numerous to mention. We benefited tremendously by attending and learning from discussions at meetings of the National Assessment Governing Board and meetings of its contractors; we thank them for opening their meetings to us and for sharing their knowledge and perspectives. We extend thanks to the staff of the cognitive laboratories and of Harcourt Brace Educational Measurement and Riverside Publishing for access to important information and their perspectives throughout the course of our work.

We relied heavily on the input and advice of a cadre of testing and disciplinary experts, who provided helpful and insightful presentations at our workshops: they are listed in Appendices A-C, and we thank them. Our work was enriched by the stimulating intellectual exchange at the meetings to which they contributed greatly.

William Morrill, Rebecca Adamson, and Donald Wise of Mathtech, Inc., provided important help and perspective throughout. They attended and reported on workshops, cognitive laboratories, and bias review sessions, provided important insight into VNT development, and were valuable members of the evaluation team.

This report has been reviewed by individuals chosen for their diverse perspectives and technical expertise, in accordance with procedures approved by the Report Review Committee of the National Research Council (NRC). The purpose of this independent review is to provide candid and critical comments that will assist the authors and the NRC in making the published report as sound as possible and to ensure that the report meets institutional standards for objectivity, evidence, and responsiveness to the study charge. The content of the review comments and draft manuscript remain confidential to protect the integrity of the deliberative process.

We wish to thank the following individuals, who are neither officials nor employees of the NRC, for their participation in the review of this report: Arthur S. Goldberger, Department of Economics, University of Wisconsin; Lyle V. Jones, L.L. Thurstone Psychometric Laboratory, University of North Carolina, Chapel Hill; Michael J. Kolen, Iowa Testing Programs, University of Iowa; Henry W. Riecken, Professor of Behavioral Sciences (emeritus), University of Pennsylvania School of Medicine; Alan H. Schoenfeld, School of Education, University of California, Berkeley; Richard Shavelson, School of Education, Stanford University; Ross M. Stolzenberg, Department of Sociology, University of Chicago. Although these individuals provided many constructive comments and suggestions, responsibility for the final content of this report rests solely with the authors and the NRC.

Above all, we are grateful to the many individuals at the National Research Council who provided guidance and assistance at many stages of the evaluation and during the preparation of the report. Barbara Torrey, executive director of the Commission on Behavioral and Social Sciences and Education (CBASSE), helped and encouraged our work—and the companion VNT studies—throughout. Sandy Wigdor, director of CBASSE's Division on Education, Labor, and Human Performance, also has been a source of great encouragement and paved many paths in the conduct of the study. We are indebted, also, to the whole CBASSE staff for indulging our scheduling exigencies. Thanks also to Sally Stanfield and the whole Audubon team at the National Academy Press, for their creative and speedy support.

We are especially grateful to Eugenia Grohman, associate director for reports of CBASSE, for her advice on structuring the content of the report, for her expert editing of the manuscript, for her wise advice on the exposition of the report's main messages, and for her patient and deft guidance of the report through the NRC review process.

We also are immensely grateful to Stephen Baldwin, Patricia Morison, and Naomi Chudowsky of the BOTA staff and Marilyn Dabady, a Yale Ph.D. candidate and BOTA summer intern, who made valuable contributions to our research and report.

We express our gratitude to NRC administrative staff Adrienne Carrington and Lisa Alston. We are especially grateful to Dorothy Majewski and Viola Horek, who capably and admirably managed the operational aspects of the evaluation—arranging meeting and workshop logistics, producing multiple iterations of drafts and report text, and being available to assist with our requests, however large or small.

We recognize the special contributions of Michael Feuer, BOTA director, and Karen Mitchell, senior staff officer, as our coauthors of this report. Michael guided the project, coordinated our work with the companion VNT projects on linkage and appropriate test use, and, most important, made frequent contributions to the discussion and the framing of our questions and conclusions. Karen was a principal source of expertise in both the substance and process of the evaluation, and she provided cheerful and continuous liaison between the two of us and the staff of NAGB and AIR. Without her help, we could not have completed our work in time and to the NRC's rigorous standards.

Lastly, we thank Winnie and Tess for their patience, help, understanding, and good humor during our work on this project. We'll be home for dinner.

Lauress Wise and Robert Hauser,
Co-Principal Investigators
Evaluation of the Voluntary National Tests

Contents

Executive Summary 1

1 The Proposed Voluntary National Tests and Their Evaluation 5

2 Test Specifications 12

3 Item Development and Review 17

4 VNT Pilot and Field Test Plans 35

5 Inclusion and Accommodation 45

6 Reporting 48

References 52

Appendices
- A Workshop on Item and Test Specifications for VNT 57
- B Workshop to Review VNT Pilot and Field Test Plans 59
- C Workshop on VNT Item Development 60
- D Source Documents 62
- E Descriptions of Achievement Levels for Basic, Proficient, and Advanced 63
- F Revised Item Development and Review Schedule for VNT 66
- G Observations of Cognitive Labs and Bias Reviews 70
- H Biographical Sketches 72

Public Law 105-78, enacted November 13, 1997

SEC. 308. STUDY—The National Academy of Sciences shall, not later than September 1, 1998, submit a written report to the Committee on Education and the Workforce of the House of Representatives, the Committee on Labor and Human Resources of the Senate, and the Committees on Appropriations of the House and Senate that evaluates all test items developed or funded by the Department of Education or any other agency of the Federal Government pursuant to contract RJ97153001, any subsequent contract related thereto, or any contract modification by the National Assessment Governing Board pursuant to section 307 of this Act, for—

(1) the technical quality of any test items for 4th grade reading and 8th grade mathematics;
(2) the validity, reliability, and adequacy of developed test items;
(3) the validity of any developed design which links test results to student performance;
(4) the degree to which any developed test items provide valid and useful information to the public;
(5) whether the test items are free from racial, cultural, or gender bias;
(6) whether the test items address the needs of disadvantaged, limited English proficient and disabled students; and
(7) whether the test items can be used for tracking, graduation or promotion of students.

Executive Summary

In his 1997 State of the Union address, President Clinton announced a federal initiative to develop tests of 4th-grade reading and 8th-grade mathematics that would provide reliable information about student performance at two key points in their educational careers. According to the U.S. Department of Education, the Voluntary National Tests (VNT) would create a catalyst for continued school improvement by focusing parental and community-wide attention on achievement and would become new tools to hold school systems accountable for their students' performance. The National Assessment Governing Board (NAGB) has responsibility for development of the VNT.

The tests would be voluntary because the federal government would prepare but not require them, and no individual, school, or group data would be reported to the federal government. Every effort would be made to include and accommodate students with disabilities and English-language learners in the testing program. The tests would provide sufficiently reliable information so all students—and their parents and teachers—would know where they stood in relation to high national standards and, in mathematics, also in relation to levels of achievement in other countries.

In order to provide maximum preparation and feedback to students, parents, and teachers, sample tests would be circulated in advance, and copies of the original tests would be returned with the original and correct answers marked. A major effort would be made to communicate test results clearly to students, parents, and teachers, and all test items would be released on the Internet just after each test was administered.

Congress recognized that a testing program of the scale and magnitude of the VNT initiative raises many important technical questions and requires quality control throughout development and implementation. In P.L. 105-78, Congress called on the National Research Council (NRC) to evaluate a series of technical issues pertaining to the validity of test items, the validity of proposed links between the VNT and the National Assessment of Educational Progress (NAEP), plans for the accommodation and inclusion of students with disabilities and English-language learners, plans for reporting test information to parents and the public, and potential uses of the tests. (Congress also requested two additional studies, one on the linkage and equivalency of tests and the other on appropriate test use.)

In accepting this charge, the NRC appointed us co-principal investigators. Working closely with NRC staff and consultants, under the auspices and oversight of the NRC's Board on Testing and Assessment, we have solicited a wide range of expert advice, conducted a number of data-gathering and analytical activities, and held three public workshops.

This report covers phase 1 of the evaluation (November 1997-July 1998) and focuses on three principal issues: test specifications and frameworks; preliminary evidence of the quality of test items; and plans for the pilot and field test studies, for inclusion and accommodation, and for reporting VNT results.

TEST SPECIFICATIONS

The VNT test specifications are appropriately based on NAEP frameworks and specifications, but they are incomplete. The close correspondence with NAEP builds on NAEP efforts to achieve a consensus on important reading and mathematical knowledge and skills and maximizes the prospects for linking VNT scores to NAEP achievement levels. However, the current test specifications lack information on test difficulty and accuracy targets and they are not yet sufficiently tied to the achievement-level descriptions that will be used in reporting. Some potential users also question the decision to test only in English.

We recommend that test difficulty and accuracy targets and additional information on the NAEP achievement-level descriptions be added to the test specifications. We also recommend that NAGB work to build a greater consensus for the test specifications to maximize participation by all school districts and states.

TEST ITEMS

Because of significant time pressures, several item review and revision steps have been conducted simultantously, and opportunities have been missed to incorporate feedback from individual steps. Yet relative to professional and scientific standards of test construction, the development of VNT items to date has been satisfactory, especially in light of the significant time pressures. NAGB and its consortium of contractors and subcontractors have made good progress toward the goal of developing a VNT item pool of adequate size and of known, high quality. While we cannot determine in advance whether that goal will be met, we find that the procedures and plans for item development and evaluation are sound. The hurried pace also prevented full development of an item tracking system.

The VNT test design presented some novel problems for which there are no ready solutions. For example, the compressed schedule did not permit the fundamental development work that would be required to ensure both inclusion and comparable validity of test scores for students who are English-language learners and students with disabilities.

In addition, the design of the tests and of their results has continued to evolve during the development process. For example, while the goal of reporting in terms of achievement levels has remained constant, there has as yet been no decision about the possibility of reporting scaled scores or ranges of scores as well. Indeed, some features of test design, such as test length, appear to have been determined administratively, ignoring possible implications for the validity or reliability of the test.

We recommend that NAGB allow more time for future test development cycles so that the different review activities can be performed sequentially rather than in parallel. We also recommend that NAGB and its contractor develop a more automated item-tracking system

so as to have timely information on survival rates and the need for additional items. Item development should be tracked by content and format categories and by link to achievement-level descriptions so that shortages of any particular type of item can be quickly identified.

PILOT AND FIELD TEST PLANS

The pilot and field test plans appear generally sound with respect to the number of items and forms to be included and the composition and size of the samples. More detail on plans for data analysis is needed and some aspects of the design, such as the use of hybrid forms, appear unnecessarily complex.

We recommend that NAGB and its contractor develop more specific plans for the analysis and use of both the pilot and field test data. These plans should include decision rules for item screening and accuracy targets for item parameter estimates, test equating, and linking. We also recommend that greater justification be supplied for some aspects of these plans, such as the use of hybrid forms, or that specific complexities be eliminated. NAGB should also prepare back-up plans in case item survival rates following the pilot test are significantly lower than anticipated.

INCLUSION AND ACCOMMODATION

Plans for including and accommodating students with disabilities and English-language learners are sketchy and do not yet break new ground with respect to maximizing the degree of inclusion and the validity of scores for all students.

We recommend that NAGB accelerate its plans and schedule for inclusion and accommodation of students with disabilities and limited English proficiency in order to increase both the participation of those student populations and to increase the comparability of VNT performance among student populations.

REPORTING PLANS

There are a number of potential issues in the reporting of test results to parents, students, and teachers that should be resolved as soon as possible, including: the adequacy of VNT items for reporting in relation to the NAEP achievement-level descriptions; mechanisms for communicating uncertainty in the results; and ways to accurately aggregate scores across student populations. We also question whether and how additional information might be provided to parents, students, and teachers for students found to be in the "below basic" category.

We recommend that NAGB accelerate its specification of procedures for reporting because reporting goals should drive most other aspects of test development. Specific consideration should be given to whether and how specific test items will be linked and used to illustrate the achievement-level descriptions. Attention should also be given to how measurement error and other sources of variation will be communicated to users, how scores will be aggregated, and whether information beyond achievement-level categories can be provided, particularly for students below the basic level of achievement.

1

The Proposed Voluntary National Tests and Their Evaluation

Standards-based reform is the centerpiece of recent efforts to improve primary and secondary education in the United States. The basic idea is that creating and aligning new, high standards for curriculum, instruction, and assessment for all students at every grade level will raise academic performance. Provisions in the 1994 reauthorization of Title I of the Elementary and Secondary Education Act, the Goals 2000 legislation, and the new Individuals with Disabilities Education Act (IDEA) all support and prompt standards-based education reform. Most states have or are developing both challenging standards for student performance and assessments that measure student performance against those standards.

Most state assessments provide information about the performance of schools and school districts, as well as individual students. However, there is no common scale that permits comparisons of student (or school) performance in different states with nationwide standards, like those of the National Assessment of Educational Progress (NAEP), or with the performance of students in other countries as indicated by the Third International Mathematics and Science Study (TIMSS). A new study from the National Research Council (1999c) concludes that it would not be feasible to develop such a common scale or to link individual score reports from existing tests to NAEP. In addition, a recent report by the U.S. General Accounting Office (GAO, 1998) explored reasons for discrepancies among states in the percentage of students who show satisfactory levels of achievement and the role that the Voluntary National Tests (VNT) might play in reducing these discrepancies.

PROPOSED TESTS

In his 1997 State of the Union address, President Clinton announced a federal initiative to develop tests of 4th-grade reading and 8th-grade mathematics that could be administered on a voluntary basis by states and school districts beginning in spring 1999. The call for VNT echoed a similar proposal for "America's Test," which the Bush administration offered in 1990. The principal purpose of the VNT, as articulated by the Secretary of the U.S. Department of Education (see, e.g., Riley, 1997), is to provide parents and teachers with systematic and reliable information about the key verbal and quantitative skills that students have achieved at two key points in their educational careers. The U.S. Department of Education anticipates that this information will serve as a catalyst for continued school improvement, by focusing parental and communitywide attention on achievement and by providing an additional tool to hold school systems accountable for their students' performance in relation to nationwide standards.

The proposed VNT has evolved in many ways since January 1997, but the major features were clear in the initial plan. Achievement tests in English reading at the 4th-grade level and in mathematics at the 8th-grade level would be offered to states, school districts, and localities for administration in the spring of each school year. Other features include:

- The tests would be voluntary because the federal government would prepare but not require them, nor would data on any individual, school, or group be reported to the federal government.
- The tests would be distributed and scored through licensed commercial firms.
- A major effort would be made to include and accommodate English-language learners and students with disabilities in the testing program.
- The tests, each administered in two, 45-minute sessions in a single day, would not be long or detailed enough to provide diagnostic information about individual learning problems. However, they would provide reliable information so all students—and their parents and teachers—would know where they are in relation to high national standards and, in mathematics, in comparison with levels of achievement in other countries.
- The tests would be designed to facilitate linkage with the National Assessment of Educational Progress (NAEP) and the reporting of individual test performance in terms of the NAEP achievement levels: basic, proficient, and advanced.
- For the 4th-grade reading test, the standards would be set by the achievement levels of the corresponding tests of NAEP.
- For the 8th-grade mathematics test, corresponding standards would be set by the 8th-grade mathematics tests of NAEP. Comparisons with achievement in other countries would be provided by linking to results from the Third International Mathematics and Science Study.
- In order to provide maximum preparation and feedback to students, parents, and teachers, sample tests would be circulated in advance, and copies of the original tests would be returned with the students' original and correct answers noted.
- A major effort would be made to communicate test results clearly to students, parents, and teachers, and all test items would be published on the Internet just after the administration of each test.

The VNT proposal does not suggest any direct use of VNT scores to make high-stakes decisions about individual students, that is, about tracking, promotion, or graduation. Representatives of the U.S. Department of Education have stated that the VNT is not intended for use in making such decisions, and the test is not being developed to support such uses. Nonetheless, some civil rights organizations and other groups have expressed concern that test users would inappropriately use VNT scores for these purposes. Indeed, under the plan, test users (states, school districts, or schools) would be free to use the tests as they wish, just as test users are now free to use commercial tests for purposes other than those recommended by their developers and publishers. A new National Research Council report (1999b:Ch.12) concludes: "The VNT should not be used for decisions about the tracking, promotion, or graduation of individual students." The VNT plan also does not preclude the possibility that the VNT would be used for aggregate accountability purposes at the level of schools, school districts, or states.

EVALUATION PLAN

A testing program of the scale and magnitude of the VNT initiative raises many important technical questions and calls for quality control throughout the various stages of development and implementation. Public debate over the merits of the program began even before any evaluation of the technical adequacy of the test design or content or administration would have been possible (see, e.g., Applebome, 1997). There are strong differences of opinion, for example, over such issues as the appropriate roles for federal, state, and local authorities in developing and governing such a program; probable and possible consequences of the tests on teaching and learning; efficacy for minority students, disadvantaged students, students with disabilities, and English-language learners; the quality of the information that the tests will provide to the public; the relationship of the tests to other state, local, national, and even international assessment programs; and the general concept of using standardized tests as a major tool for educational accountability.

Policy debates are at times difficult to disentangle from arguments over technical properties of testing programs. The overall purpose of this evaluation is to focus on the technical adequacy and quality of the development, administration, scoring, reporting, and uses of the VNT. Through procedures designed to assure rigorous and impartial scientific evaluation of the available data, we have attempted to provide information about VNT development that will aid test developers and policy makers at the federal, state, and local levels. This phase 1 report focuses on: (1) specifications for the 4th-grade reading and 8th-grade mathematics tests, (2) the development and review of items for the tests, and (3) plans for subsequent test-development activities. The last includes plans for the pilot and field tests, for inclusion and accommodation of students with disabilities and English-language learners, and for scoring and reporting the tests. Note that we interpret our mandate as a request for technical review only, and we take no position on the overall merits of the VNT.

Initial plans for the evaluation of the VNT, developed at the request of the Department of Education in late summer 1997, followed the department's initial schedule for the design, validation, and implementation of the tests. Following President Clinton's January 1997 State of the Union address, the schedule called for development of test specifications for 4th-grade reading and 8th-grade mathematics tests by fall 1997, pilot testing of test items later that year, and field testing of test forms early in 1998. The first test administration was slated for spring 1999. Subsequent negotiations between the administration and Congress, which culminated in passage of the fiscal 1998 appropriations bill (P.L. 105-78), led to a suspension of test item development (a stop-work order) late in September 1997 and transferred to the National Assessment Governing Board (NAGB, the governing body for NAEP) exclusive authority to oversee the policies, direction, and guidelines for developing the VNT. The law gave NAGB 90 days in which to review the development plan and the contract with a private consortium, led by the American Institutes for Research (AIR), for the development work.

Congress further instructed NAGB to make four determinations about the VNT:

(1) the extent to which test items selected for use on the tests are free from racial, cultural, or gender bias;

(2) whether the test development process and test items adequately assess student reading and

mathematics comprehension in the form most likely to yield accurate information regarding student achievement in reading and mathematics;

(3) whether the test development process and test items take into account the needs of disadvantaged, limited-English-proficient, and students with disabilities; and

(4) whether the test development process takes into account how parents, guardians, and students will appropriately be informed about testing content, purpose, and uses.

NAGB negotiated a revised schedule and work plan with AIR. It calls for test development over a 3-year period—with pilot testing in March 1999, field testing in March 2000, and operational test administration in March 2001. In addition, the work plan specifies a major decision point in fall 1998, which depends on congressional action, and it permits limited test-development activities to proceed through the remainder of the fiscal year, to September 30, 1998.

When the Congress assigned NAGB responsibility for the VNT, it also called on the National Research Council (NRC) to evaluate the technical adequacy of test materials. Specifically, it asked the NRC to evaluate:

(1) the technical quality of any test items for 4th-grade reading and 8th-grade mathematics;

(2) the validity, reliability, and adequacy of developed test items;

(3) the validity of any developed design which links test results to student performance levels;

(4) the degree to which any developed test items provide valid and useful information to the public;

(5) whether the test items are free from racial, cultural, or gender bias;

(6) whether the test items address the needs of disadvantaged, limited-English-proficient, and disabled students; and

(7) whether the test items can be used for tracking, graduation, or promotion of students.

To carry out this mandate (specified in P.L. 105-78 [Sections 305-311], November 1997), the NRC appointed us as co-principal investigators. We have worked with NRC staff under the auspices and oversight of the NRC's Board on Testing and Assessment (BOTA) and solicited input from a wide range of outside experts.

The congressional charges to NAGB and to the NRC were constrained by P.L. 105-78 requirements that "no funds . . . may be used to field test, pilot test, administer or distribute in any way, any national tests" and that the NRC report be delivered by September 1, 1998. The plan for pilot testing in March 1999 required that a large pool of potential VNT items be developed, reviewed, and approved by late fall of 1998, to provide time for the construction, publication, and distribution of multiple draft test forms for the pilot test. Given the March 1998 start-up date, NAGB, its prime contractor AIR, and the subcontractors for reading and mathematics test development (Riverside Publishing and Harcourt-Brace Educational Measurement) have faced a daunting and compressed schedule for test design and development, and we have been able to observe only a part of the item development process (and not its final products). Moreover, because preliminary testing and statistical analyses of test data are essential steps in the development and evaluation of new tests, our evaluation is necessarily preliminary and incomplete.

We offer substantial, but preliminary, evidence about three of the seven issues in the congressional mandate to the NRC: (1) technical quality; (2) validity; and (5) bias. These correspond to the first and second determinations to be made by NAGB, freedom from bias and accuracy of information. We have also sought evidence about the other important issues raised in the congressional mandate. Our discussion of them, except the last—"high-stakes" use of test items, that is, for tracking, graduation, or promotion of students—is even more preliminary and is, in large part, limited to an evaluation of the NAGB and AIR plans for the subsequent stages of test development. As noted above, another congressionally mandated study of the VNT concludes that the VNT should not be used for decisions about tracking, promotion, or graduation (National Research Council, 1999b), and we concur in that recommendation. We cannot address the remaining issues definitively unless test development continues into the pilot phase and empirical data on item performance are available for analyses.

We note that our charge did not include cost issues, and we did not endeavor to examine probable costs for the VNT. Issues of cost are addressed by a recent report on the VNT by the U.S. General Accounting Office (1998).

EVALUATION ACTIVITIES

In this phase of the VNT evaluation, we have focused largely on three aspects of the test development process and products: issues surrounding the test specifications and the NAEP frameworks; plans for the development and implementation of the pilot study, scheduled for spring 1999; and preliminary evidence of the quality of possible test items. To date, we have observed laboratory-based talk-aloud item tryout sessions with students, reviewed design and development plans and reports, examined draft test items and scoring materials, and conducted three workshops at which additional experts with a wide range of skills and experience have contributed unique and invaluable input. (See Appendices A-C for lists of the expert participants in each workshop.)

Our December 1997 workshop reviewed test specifications and linking plans. This meeting occurred prior to the revision of the NAGB and AIR workplan. The workshop enabled us and the NRC staff to review and assess the previously developed test specifications in relation to the NAEP mathematics and reading frameworks. The workshop also reviewed issues in test equating and linkage that would be relevant to the evaluation of linkages of the VNT in reading and mathematics with corresponding NAEP instruments, as well as to the mission of the Committee on Equivalency and Linkage of Educational Tests (see National Research Council, 1999c). We believe that the workshop helped to inform the subsequent modification of development plans by NAGB.

Our second workshop in April 1998 reviewed pilot and field test plans. At that time, the revised development work plan was in place, and item development had resumed. The goal of this workshop was to review the contractors' plans for collecting and analyzing empirical data about the items and subsequent test forms after initial development was complete. The proceedings of that meeting, along with our review of the NAGB and AIR plans and revisions, have been very helpful in our evaluation.

For our June 1998 workshop, we led an expert review of item quality, based on a sample of reading and mathematics items that had been developed as of that date. We planned the workshop to take place late enough in the development process so we could base this report on tangible evidence of item quality but early enough for us to produce the report in a timely fashion. In fact, as described below, the workshop yielded evidence that the item development schedule did not allow enough time for item review and revision and that there might be inadequate numbers of certain types of items. We issued an interim letter report on July 16, 1998 (National Research Council, 1998), which recommended changes in the item review and revision schedule and possible development of additional items within the overall constraint of approval of the item pool by NAGB in late fall 1998. We summarize the findings and recommendations from that report below, along with subsequent modifications of the development plan and schedule by NAGB and the AIR consortium.

The evaluation of draft items by AIR in one-on-one think-aloud sessions with 4th- and 8th-graders during May and June 1998—called cognitive laboratories—was a significant and innovative item development activity. The sessions were carried out as a complement to, and simultaneously with, other review processes, including professional content reviews by AIR and its subcontractors and bias and sensitivity reviews led by the subcontractors. The cognitive labs are a potentially valuable tool for test development, providing direct feedback to the developers about student understanding of items. For that reason we looked closely at the design and conduct of the labs and, in a more limited way, at the use of information from the labs in item review and revision. We also observed the bias and sensitivity reviews.

REPORT OVERVIEW AND THEMES

Ideally, if the test development process were fully informed by the desired properties of the tests and of test results and if there were no other time or resource constraints, one would expect a process whose steps were geared precisely to standards for the targeted outcomes. For example, VNT results are to be reported primarily in terms of NAEP achievement levels, so those levels should inform the specification and development of the item pool. For the same reason, the length of the test should be sufficient to ensure a range of accuracy in reports of test results that would be understandable and informative to students, parents, and teachers. The goals of inclusion and accommodation of English-language learners and students with disabilities suggest the desirability of developing a test from the beginning with tasks that are accessible to all students and whose results are comparable among all students—with or without accommodation. Finally, the pilot and field test plans would yield exactly the data needed to address the problems of test construction, reliable estimation, freedom from bias, and comparability among all major populations of students.

The VNT development process does not entirely meet these standards, but—relative to current professional and scientific standards of test construction—it has been satisfactory. That is, NAGB and its consortium of contractors and subcontractors have made a great deal of progress toward the goal of developing a VNT item pool of adequate size and of known, high quality. While we cannot determine in advance whether that goal will be met, we do find that the procedures and plans for item development and evaluation are sound. If the development process continues through pilot and field testing, we expect there will be clear answers about the size and quality of the item pool; the reliability, fairness, and validity of items; the accessibility and comparability of the tests for students with low English proficiency or disabilities; and the linkages among alternative test forms and of those test forms with NAEP and TIMSS. We can imagine that there might have been much less satisfactory outcomes at this stage of test development, and progress to date is no small achievement.

There are, however, understandable reasons why the test development process has not met the highest possible standards. First, as we have already stated, the schedule has been somewhat compressed, relative to the usual time allowed for item development. There is some compensation for the compressed schedule in the fact that the test specifications are very similar to those of NAEP and that test development has been informed by the experience of NAEP item development.

Second, the test design presented some novel problems for which there are no ready solutions. For example, the compressed schedule did not permit the fundamental development work that would be required to assure both inclusion and comparable validity of test scores for students with disabilities or those with limited English proficiency (see National Research Council, 1999b). Consequently, the developers chose to leave issues of inclusion and accommodation mainly untouched until completion of the pilot test. Furthermore, while NAEP provides some good experience in reporting specific achievement levels, the fact that test results are not reported for individual students in NAEP makes that task for VNT much more complex. In the case of the VNT, students, parents, and teachers will be able to compare actual test items with nominal achievement levels in the context of individual student performance, and this creates demands for face validity that do not exist in NAEP. Again, the developers appear to have used standard procedures for item development, leaving the match between potential items and achievement-level descriptions for a later phase of the development process.

Third, the design of the tests and of their results has continued to evolve during the development process. For example, while the goal of reporting in terms of achievement levels has remained constant, there has so far been no decision about the possibility of also reporting scaled scores or ranges of scores. There has also been no decision about whether and how information will be provided for students below the basic achievement level.

Fourth, the test development team is new, and its division of labor between NAGB and the prime contractor and between the prime and subcontractors is complex. Under these circumstances—essentially a trial run—one might well expect (and we have observed) less than perfect coordination of procedures, activities, and materials among development activities.

Finally, some features of test design appear to have been determined administratively, ignoring possible implications for the validity or reliability of the test. For example, test length appears to have been determined in advance by beliefs about the potential test-taking burden. Experiments with existing subsets of NAEP items could be informative about test length, relative to desired accuracy, in various types of reports of student performance.

Again, if the development process continues and the later stages go as planned, these problems may not jeopardize the quality of the final products of this round of VNT development. If the VNT program continues beyond the first round of development and testing, these issues should be addressed in later cycles of test development and evaluation. When the goals and products of the program are more clearly defined and the several partners of the development consortium gain experience in working together, the test development process will probably become better aligned to the program's planned outcomes.

Since item development for the VNT is still at an early stage, part of our review focused on plans for future activities, including: (1) further item review; (2) the pilot test; (3) the field test, with plans for equating and linking; (4) test administration, including accomodations for English-language learners and students with disabilities; and (5) reporting plans. In each area, we found several issues that will need attention if the program is to succeed. Without timely attention to these concerns, future progress is unlikely to be satisfactory.

The remainder of the report is in five chapters, each of which pertains to a major phase of test development: test specifications; item development, review, and revision; pilot and field test plans; inclusion and accommodation; and reporting. Of these development activities, only the first is now complete. We have a lot of evidence about item development and review activities, but the schedule precludes our complete evaluation of the item pool or draft test forms developed for the pilot test. In the case of the other three phases of development, we have assessed plans as of mid-July 1998. Our findings, conclusions, and recommendations are based on both input from the experts and other participants at our three workshops and our analysis and assessment of the published materials cited throughout this report and other documents made available to us by NAGB and AIR (see Appendix D).

2

Test Specifications

Specifications for the Voluntary National Tests (VNT) were originally developed in October 1997 by the Council of Chief State School Officers (CCSSO) and MPR Associates, Inc., under contract to the U.S. Department of Education (Council of Chief State Schools Officers and MPR Associates, 1997a; 1997b). Responsibility for developing and approving test specifications was transferred to the National Assessment Governing Board (NAGB) under P.L. 105-78. NAGB established a Test Specifications Committee with separate reading and mathematics subcommittees. This committee commissioned several expert reviews of the test specifications and held public hearings in January 1998 in Washington, D.C., and Chicago, Illinois. Its recommendations for revised specifications were offered to NAGB, which spent much of its March 1998 meeting reviewing and revising those recommendations in a committee of the whole. At the conclusion of its meeting, NAGB approved an outline of the specifications as amended (National Assessment Governing Board, 1998a; 1998b).

NAGB's specifications for VNT say that each test is to be taken in two 45-minute sessions on the same day. About 80 percent of the reading and mathematics items, but only one-half the testing period, is to be administered in a multiple-choice format. The remaining items in each test are to be constructed-response items, some requiring short answers and others requiring extended responses. Eighth-grade students are to be provided with manipulatives (ruler, protractor, and geometric shapes) throughout the examination and with an electronic calculator during the second session of the examination. However, the test is designed so that calculators will be of no use in about one-third of the items in that session, and the remaining items are to be divided between those for which a calculator would be required (labeled "calculator active") and those for which a calculator would be useful but not essential (labeled "calculator neutral").

The primary differences between the October 1997 and March 1998 versions of the VNT specifications are in (1) the resemblance between the reading and mathematics specifications and the corresponding National Assessment of Educational Progress (NAEP) frameworks; (2) the level of detail provided in the specifications; (3) the absence of non-English forms of the reading test; (4) the inclusion of intertextual items in reading (questions that ask students to compare or contrast two text passages); and (5) details on calculator use and item response format in mathematics. The March 1998 VNT specifications depart minimally from the corresponding NAEP specifications, mainly as required to yield individual student scores. For example, in 4th-grade reading, the text passages are shorter than in NAEP, and intertextual items may permit the introduction of more questions without the need to add reading passages. Unlike the October specifications, the March specifications exist only in outline form, and item developers have been referred to current NAEP frameworks for more complete information about item content, difficulty, and structure (National Assessment Governing Board, no date[a], no date[b]). Again, the March specifications reflect several important decisions about the VNT: that the reading test would be offered only in English; that it might include some intertextual items; that the mathematics test would be split between sections where calculator use is prohibited and permitted; and that some open-ended mathematics items would require responses that need to be drawn or entered on a grid (which can be machine scored but requires students to supply an answer rather than respond to a list of options).

FINDINGS

First, our overall finding about the test specifications for VNT is that the test specifications provide a reasonable but incomplete basis for item development. This finding is based on our judgments about (1) the appropriateness of using the NAEP frameworks as the primary basis for the VNT test specifications, (2) the acceptance of VNT specifications by educators and policy makers, and (3) the completeness of the specifications outlines.

Appropriateness

The test specifications, as amended and approved by NAGB, are nearly identical to the NAEP specifications with respect to the knowledge and skills to be measured. The VNT specifications are also similar to NAEP specifications for item formats, although a slightly different mix is required to support scores for individual students. The similarity with NAEP also extends to other issues, such as the provision of calculators during part of the test. There are a few exceptions, such as the use of intertextual items in reading and the use of gridded and drawn responses in mathematics. Such divergences are likely to be temporary, however, as these innovations may also be introduced into NAEP in the near future.

The NAEP test frameworks that are used as the primary basis for the VNT were developed by a careful consensus process, incorporating input from diverse groups and relying heavily on national professional groups outside the federal government. For the most part, the frameworks steer a middle course through special interest groups that seek to emphasize narrower perspectives on reading and mathematics. In reading, the skills that are emphasized range from demonstrating an understanding of individual words through critical evaluation of text. Similarly, the mathematics skills needed range from simple computation through application of advanced problem-solving skills.

A key feature of NAEP, which is carried into the VNT specifications, is its lack of alignment with any particular curriculum or instructional approach. This approach avoids infringement on local and state responsibilities for curriculum and pedagogical decisions, but it also limits somewhat the potential uses of the VNT. Specifically, before the VNT is used to assess teachers, schools, or individual students, it will be important to understand the degree of alignment of the instructional program to which students are exposed and the knowledge and skills assessed in NAEP and the VNT.

Acceptance

Second, we observe that there is a lack of broad acceptance of the final test specifications. For example, a number of school districts withdrew from the VNT program when it was decided that the 4th-grade reading test would be in English only. Also, a significant number of educators want greater emphasis on the basic skills (e.g., decoding and computation) that, in theory, must be mastered before students can reach the basic achievement level. Other educators seek greater attention to more complex thinking and reasoning skills (see, e.g., Resnick, 1987). A broader consensus for current decisions may increase eventual participation rates for VNT. (See National Research Council, 1999b, for a discussion of public discourse and its role in testing policy.)

Completeness

Third, while the VNT specifications provide a reasonable basis for item development, they lack information about statistical targets for items and forms that characterize most test specifications and that are needed for building test forms. In addition, the specifications lack specific information on the NAEP achievement-level descriptions to be used in reporting VNT results and about possible additional reporting scales. Also absent are goals for the assessment of English-language learners and students with disabilities.

We note that most test specifications include targets for item difficulty or specify overall test score accuracy targets (or both). While the VNT specifications include targets for length and number of items of various types, they do not specify either the form in which performance will be reported—beyond reference to NAEP achievement levels—or the accuracy with which those reports are to be made at varying levels of achievement.

As noted in our interim report (National Research Council, 1998), as of July the contractors had not yet begun to relate VNT items to the descriptions of the NAEP achievement levels that will be used in reporting VNT results (see Appendix E). These descriptions list the knowledge and skills that students must exhibit to be classified at particular levels of achievement. Given NAGB's strong support for achievement-level reporting, we think it is unfortunate that the VNT test specifications do not contain the achievement-level descriptions. The test specifications, available only in outline form, reference the NAEP 1996 mathematics and 1992 reading frameworks for detail on test content. Neither of these documents, however, contains the text of the achievement-level descriptions. We also examined copies of the materials used to train VNT item writers. The text of the achievement-level descriptions was found only in training materials for reading, and there was no mention of the implications of these descriptions for items. Furthermore, the specifications omit discussion of possible additional reporting scales for the VNT.

Also absent from the VNT specifications are goals for the inclusion and accommodation of students with disabilities and English-language learners. Briefly, as required by law, students with special needs should be included in the VNT (as in other testing programs) to the maximum extent possible, and the VNT should be designed to yield performance estimates for them—after necessary accommodation—that will be comparable with and as valid and reliable as those for other students. In the case of the VNT, the developers have assumed that adequate provisions for inclusion and accommodation can be introduced, following recent NAEP practice, at a later stage of the development process (see Chapter 5).

CONCLUSIONS

By using the NAEP specifications, the VNT can build on important efforts to develop a national consensus on what students should know and be able to do, rather than try to reinvent such a consensus. The use of NAEP frameworks also means that test developers have access to a wide array of released NAEP items as relevant examples. Another benefit of the close resemblance of VNT specifications to NAEP is an increased likelihood of constructing valid linkages between levels of performance on the VNT and the NAEP achievement levels. To be sure, this will require additional work relating the VNT item pool to NAEP achievement levels, as noted in our interim report (National Research Council, 1998), as well as careful statistical work with the pilot and field test forms. Further discussion of this issue appears below and in *Uncommon Measures: Equivalence and Linkage Among Educational Tests* (National Research Council, 1999c).

As we noted above, however, the consensus achieved in the VNT specifications is well short of universal assent, and attention might well be paid to areas of continuing disagreement. There is no consensus about the need for non-English forms or about the appropriate balance of attention to basic and more complex skills in the VNT.

In addition, we note that the specifications lack important information about target difficulty levels for items and forms They address the NAEP achievement levels only minimally and lack full information about intended reporting scales for VNT. The specifications also omit sponsors' and developers' goals for inclusion and accommodation for English-language learning students and students with disabilities.

Given these omissions, it is difficult to judge the likely accuracy of student classifications in the four groups defined by the NAEP achievement levels—below basic, basic, proficient, and advanced—or whether the classifications will be equally reliable at every achievement level. For example, transforming a VNT test score into the NAEP achievement levels might yield the following type of report: ". . . among 100 students who performed at the same level as the student, call her Sally, 10 are likely to be in the below basic category, 60 are likely to be basic; 28 are likely to be proficient; and 2 are likely to be in the highest, or advanced category" (National Research Council, 1999c:Ch. 5). We note in Chapter 6 of this report that communication of this type of score information to students, parents, and teachers may combine problems of comprehension with excessive uncertainty.

A closely related issue—as yet unresolved by NAGB and absent in the specifications—is the possibility of reporting a scaled test score along with NAEP achievement levels. We note here and in Chapter 6 that if scaled scores are not generated and reported, the VNT will provide little or no information to the large number of students whose performance lies below the basic level. About 40 percent of students nationally and 70 to 80 percent of students in some urban areas score below the basic level on NAEP. Additional information might be especially useful to students whose performance lies below, but close to, the basic level on VNT. Representatives of the Council of the Great City Schools have called for this type of reporting. In the absence of detailed feedback to low-performing students and their parents and teachers, there is likely to be little incentive to participate in the VNT. At the same time, the decision to report a full range of scores would have implications for the distribution of test items by difficulty and thus could affect test accuracy across a range of achievement levels.

We do not believe that there is adequate evidence at present about inclusion, accommodation, or comparability in the VNT specifications. (For more detailed discussion of inclusion and accommodation issues, see Chapter 5 and National Research Council, 1999b:Chs. 8, 9.)

In sum, until issues of student classification, scaled scores, and accommodation are resolved, it is not possible to reach a fully informed judgment about the adequacy of the VNT specifications.

RECOMMENDATIONS

2-1. The test specifications should be expanded to take into account developers' objectives for reporting and reliability.

2-2. The developers should work to build a wider consensus for the final test specifications.

3

Item Development and Review

American Institutes for Research (AIR) and its subcontractors had developed a modest number of potential Voluntary National Tests (VNT) items before the stop-work order in September 1997, but item development began in earnest only after approval of the test specifications by the National Assessment Governing Board (NAGB) in March 1998. Mathematics items were drafted by Harcourt-Brace Educational Measurement; reading items were drafted by Riverside Publishing. There have been several stages of content review by AIR staff and external experts, and through the cognitive laboratories. There are also several stages of review for bias and sensitivity.

Our general finding with respect to item development is that NAGB and its contractors appear on track for a pilot test in spring 1999:

(1) A large number of items have been developed.
(2) Items have been reviewed for bias and sensitivity, and additional stages of bias review are planned.
(3) Items have passed through several stages of content review.
(4) Cognitive laboratories were introduced to the item development process.
(5) An intensive and vigorous item review and revision process is ongoing.

The rest of this chapter details our findings on each of these points.

NUMBER OF ITEMS

As of July 15, 1998, more than 3,000 items had been written for the VNT and were in various stages of review and revision. Table 3-1 shows the number of items written, in comparison to the number needed for the pilot and field tests. Current plans for the pilot test require creating 24 forms containing 45 reading items each and 18 forms containing 60 mathematics items each—a combined total of 2,160

TABLE 3-1 Number of Items Available and Required for Pilot and Field Tests

Item Status	Reading	Math	Total
Developed as of 7/15/98	1,744	1,466	3,210
Needed for Pilot Test	1,080 (24 forms)	1,080 (18 forms)	2,160
Needed for Field Test	270 (6 forms)	360 (6 forms)	630
Items Per Form	45	60	

items. Roughly two-thirds of the existing items would have to survive the review and revision process to meet the item requirements for the pilot test. Field test plans require assembly of 6 reading and 6 mathematics forms—a combined total of 630 items, roughly one-third of the items included in the pilot test. In this chapter we review the adequacy of the sample of items developed thus far for meeting the pilot test requirements. In Chapter 4, we review the pilot test requirements themselves.

As described below, each of the various review steps results in a recommendation to accept, revise, or drop an item. The quantity of items developed to date will allow one-third of the items to be dropped in one or more of the review steps. Our experience with survival rates during test development is limited to screening that incorporates empirical data. In such cases, survival rates range from 30 to 70 or even 75 percent, depending on item format, the care taken in initial review and editing, and other characteristics of the testing program. For the VNT, these figures would be comparable to the combined survival rates from item review and from the pilot test. While we do not have industry information on survival rates through the review process alone, data presented later in this chapter indicate that overall survival rates from the different reviews of the VNT items are running well above the 67 percent needed to meet pilot test requirements.

Meeting the pilot test requirements, however, is somewhat more complicated. The intention is that each pilot test form will resemble an operational form in the distribution of items by content and format categories. AIR provided us with a copy of its item tracking database that includes information on the content categories for each item initially assigned by the item writers. Each item identifier included codes that indicate the content and format categories initially assigned to that item by the item writers. For mathematics, one coding scheme was used for the items developed prior to the suspension of item writing in fall 1997 and a different scheme was used for items developed subsequently. The initial coding scheme did not include codes for calculator use and had a 1-digit year code. The revised scheme included codes for mathematical ability and power as well as calculator use, but most of the time these codes were missing.

Tables 3-2 through 3-5 show comparisons of the required and available numbers of items for each content and format category described in the test specifications for mathematics and reading, respectively. Tables 3-2 and 3-4 show requirements included in the overall test specifications approved by NAGB; Tables 3-3 and 3-5 show requirements in AIR's more detailed test plans. NAGB and AIR are currently reviewing the content classification of each of the existing items, so the results presented here are far from definitive. In addition, a mapping of items onto the National Assessment of Educational Progress (NAEP) achievement-level descriptions is also planned for completion before November 1998. Since there was no initial mapping, that breakout cannot be provided here. Also, in mathemat-

TABLE 3-2 Number of Mathematics Items by NAGB Specification Categories

Description	Percent	Number per Form	Number Needed for Pilot Test	Number Developed as of 7/15/98	Minimum Needed to Retain: Percent
By Content Strand					
A. Number, properties, and operations	25	15	270	442	61
B. Measurement	15	9	162	319	51
C. Geometry and spatial sense	20	12	216	233	93
D. Data analysis, statistics, and probability	15	9	162	207	78
E. Algebra and functions	25	15	270	265	102
By Mathematical Abilities					
C. Conceptual knowledge	33	20	360	[a]	[a]
P. Procedural knowledge	33	20	360	[a]	[a]
S. Problem solving	33	20	360	[a]	[a]
By Calculator Use					
1. Calculator active[b]	33	20	360	444	81
2. Calculator neutral[c]	17	10	180	187	96
3. Calculator inactive[d]	50	30	540	650	83
By Item Format					
Multiple choice	70	42	756	953	79
Gridded response[e]	10	6	108	164	66
Drawn[f]	[g]	[g]	[g]	20	0
Short constructed response[h]	17	10	180	274	66
Extended constructed response[i]	3	2	36	55	65

[a]Many items have not yet been classified by mathematical ability.
[b]Calculator active: items require the use of a calculator.
[c]Calculator neutral: items may or may not require the use of a calculator.
[d]Calculator inactive: items for session 1 where calculators will not be permitted.
[e]Gridded response: items require students to bubble in answers in the test booklet.
[f]Drawn: items require a drawn response.
[g]Drawn items are not included in the current test specifications.
[h]Short constructed response: items require students to briefly explain an answer and show their work.
[i]Extended constructed response: items require students to provide a more detailed answer to a question, to support their position or argument with specific information from the text.

ics, many of the items have not yet been classified into ability categories, and the classification of items into calculator use categories is tentative, at best.

Our analysis suggests that if the current item classifications hold up, additional mathematics items will be needed for the content strands in algebra and functions and probably also in geometry and spatial sense. Only 264 items are currently classified as algebra and functions items; 270 will be needed for the pilot test. For geometry and spatial sense, there are currently 233 items; 216 will be needed for the pilot test, leaving little room for rejections during review. It is also possible that more "calculator neutral" items will be needed, although it may not be difficult to move some of the calculator inactive items into this category. In reading, it seems likely that additional short literary passages will be needed

TABLE 3-3 Number of Mathematics Items by AIR Strand by Format Plan

Strand and Format[a]	Number per Form[b]	Number Needed for Pilot Test	Number Developed as of 7/15/98	Minimum Needed to Retain: Percent
A. Number, Properties, and Operations				
Multiple choice	11	198	324	61
Gridded response	2	36	45	80
Short constructed response	3	54	65	83
Extended constructed response	0	0	8	0
Total	16	288	442	65
B. Measurement				
Multiple choice	7	126	202	62
Gridded response	2	36	36	100
Short constructed response	1	18	66	27
Extended constructed response	0	0	14	0
Total	10	180	318	57
C. Geometry and Spatial Sense				
Multiple choice	7	126	123	102
Gridded response	1	18	30	60
Short constructed response	2	36	47	77
Extended constructed response	1	18	19	95
Total	11	198	219	90
D. Data Analysis, Statistics, and Probability				
Multiple choice	6	108	115	94
Gridded response	1	18	39	46
Short constructed response	2	36	43	84
Extended constructed response	0	0	7	0
Total	9	162	204	79
E. Algebra and Functions				
Multiple choice	11	198	189	105
Gridded response	0	0	14	0
Short constructed response	2	36	53	68
Extended constructed response	1	18	7	257
Total	14	252	263	96
Total				
Multiple choice	42	756	953	79
Gridded response	6	108	164	66
Short constructed response	10	180	274	66
Extended constructed response	2	36	55	66
Total	60	1,080	1,446	75

[a]The current specifications do not include drawn response items, so the 20 drawn response items developed have been excluded from this table.

[b]The AIR plan meets specifications for testing time by Strand. However, due to differences in the proportion of short and extended constructed response items within each strand, the total items for each strand shown here differ slightly from those shown in Table 3-2.

TABLE 3-4 Number of Reading Items by NAGB Specification Categories

Description	Percent	Number per Form	Number Needed for Pilot Test	Number Developed as of 7/15/98	Minimum Needed to Retain: Percent
Passages by Type and Length[a]					
Short literary[b]		1	12	11	109
Medium literary		1	12	16	75
Long literary		1	12	26	46
Short informational[c]		1	12	18	66
Medium informational		2	24	30	80
Items by Stance					
Initial understanding[d]	12	5	130	216	60
Developing an interpretation[e]	53	24	572	971	59
Reader-text connections[f]	10	5	108	158	68
Critical stance[g]	25	11	270	399	68
Total	100	45	1,080	1,744	62

[a]The NAGB specifications require 50 percent of the items to be from literary passages and 50 percent to be from informational passages. AIR has further divided passages by length.

[b]Literary passages: readers develop and extend their understanding of text by making connections to their own knowledge and ideas.

[c]Informational passages: readers establish a notion of what the text is about and maintain a focus on points of information related to the topic they have identified.

[d]Initial understanding: the reader's initial impressions or global understanding immediately after finishing the text.

[e]Developing an interpretation: the reader's ability to develop a more complete understanding or comprehension of what is read.

[f]Reader-text connections: the reader's ability to connect specific information in the text with more general information the reader may bring to bear in answering the question.

[g]Critical stance: the reader's ability to look objectively at the test and to answer questions related to the author's use of character descriptions, story elements, the clarity of information provided, and related topics.

to meet the pilot test requirements. Currently, 11 of the 101 passages approved by NAGB are short literary passages, and 12 will be required for the pilot test.

In response to our interim letter report of July 16, 1998 (National Research Council, 1998), NAGB has launched plans for supplemental item development, if more items are required. We believe the requirements for additional items will be modest. Given the speed with which a very large bank of items has already been developed, there should not be any insurmountable problem in creating the additional items needed to meet pilot test requirements in each item category. Since the items have not yet been mapped to the NAEP achievement levels, however, we have no basis for determining whether the current distribution of items appropriately reflects the knowledge and skills described for each level or whether a significant number of additional items might be needed to ensure adequate coverage at all levels.

TABLE 3-5 Number of Reading Items by AIR Passage Type by Format Plan

Type and Format	Number per Form	Number Needed for Pilot Test	Number Developed as of 7/15/98	Minimum Needed to Retain: Percent
Short Literary				
Multiple choice	5-6	120-144	126	105
Short constructed response	1	24	35	69
Extended constructed response	0	0	0	0
Total	6-7	144-168	161	97
Medium Literary				
Multiple choice	5	120	176	68
Short constructed response	1-2	24-48	56	64
Extended constructed response	0	0	0	0
Total	6-7	144-168	232	67
Long Literary				
Multiple choice	8-9	192-216	399	51
Short constructed response	1-2	24-48	104	35
Extended constructed response	1	24	41	59
Total	10-12	240-288	544	49
Short Informational				
Multiple choice	4-5	96-120	192	56
Short constructed response	1	24	57	42
Extended constructed response	0	0	2	0
Total	5-6	120-144	251	53
Medium Informational				
Multiple choice	9-10	216-240	332	69
Short constructed response	1	24	66	36
Extended constructed response	1	24	44	55
Total	11-12	264-288	442	62
Intertextual[a]				
Multiple choice	2	48	75	64
Short constructed response	1	24	39	62
Total	3	96	114	84
Total				
Multiple choice	33-37	840	1,300	65
Short constructed response	7-9	192	357	54
Extended consrtucted response	2	48	87	55
Total	45	1,080	1,744	62

[a]Items that require students to answer questions based on their reading of two passages pertaining to the same or similar topics.

BIAS AND SENSITIVITY REVIEWS

The VNT specifications provide several opportunities for bias and sensitivity reviews, which differ only slightly for reading and mathematics. For 4th-grade reading, NAGB specifies (National Assessment Governing Board, 1998b:13):

(1) The VNT contractor shall conduct a thorough bias/sensitivity review of all passages and items to ensure that they are free from gender, racial, regional, and cultural bias.

(2) Panelists convened for the contractor's bias/sensitivity review shall consist of policymakers, educators, business representatives, testing experts, and members of the general public, and shall be representative of gender, racial/ethnic, and regional groups.

(3) The Board shall review all reading passages for bias prior to final passage selection and item development.

(4) The VNT contractor shall use statistical item bias procedures (e.g., differential item functioning–DIF analysis), as data become available, to augment the judgmental bias/sensitivity review.

(5) The Board shall review all VNT passages and items at various stages of development to ensure that such passages and items are bias-free.

The specifications for bias and sensitivity review of mathematics items are identical, except there is no need for NAGB preclearance of reading passages. At the present time, final NAGB review of the reading and mathematics items has not yet taken place, and—in advance of the pilot test—it is not possible to carry out the DIF (differential item functioning) analyses (see Chapter 4).

As noted above, we observed the external reviews for bias and sensitivity. Riverside Publishing convened the review of reading items in Chicago, Illinois, on July 6-8, 1998, and Harcourt-Brace Educational Measurement convened the review of mathematics items in San Antonio, Texas, on July 6-7, 1998. Each group of reviewers included about two dozen individuals from diverse groups. For example, the mathematics review group included a male American Indian, several African Americans (male and female), two Asian Americans (one male and one female), two individuals of Latin American descent, one individual who was Islamic, and one individual who was in a wheelchair. It appeared, however, that most of the reviewers were from education-related professions. For example, in the case of the reading reviewers, several were 4th-grade school teachers, and the rest were superintendents, assistant superintendents for curriculum or research, Title I coordinators, coordinators for English-language instruction programs or special education, and other education workers.

In each bias review session, the reviewers were well trained, and the staff of the publishing companies were friendly, expert, and at ease with the situation. Training materials included test specifications, a glossary of testing terms, and illustrative bias problems. Reviewers were permitted to comment on item content as well as bias problems, but most of their attention focused on bias and sensitivity issues.

Passages and items were explored from several perspectives: inappropriate language, group stereotyping, and controversial or emotionally charged topics. An effort was also made to discuss representational fairness—the inclusion of all groups in some reading passages in roles that are not stereotypical. Problems of language and stereotyping were more prevalent in the literary passages, some of which were written many years ago. Controversial or emotionally charged material—including death and disease, personal appearance, politics, religion, and unemployment—cropped up in informational as well as literary passages. Problems with mathematics items included ethnic stereotyping and the use—and overuse—of specific and sometimes nonessential commercial names in items dealing with retail purchases. Religious and ethnic differences in conventions for addressing adults—e.g., as Mr. or Mrs. or by first names—were sometimes problematic.

At both locations, the staff of the publishing companies encouraged the reviewers to report any possible problems with the items—to err on the side of excessive caution—but the percentage of items in which serious problems occurred was low. For example, in the reading review, about 5 percent of passages (though a somewhat larger percentage of specific items) were identified as problematic, and 10-15 percent of mathematics items were identified as possibly biased. We judge that the reviewers were thorough and that the review process was balanced and without doctrinaire overtones. Some passages and items were flagged for removal, but in most cases, biases could be corrected by editorial revision. However, such revision presents a nontrivial problem in the case of copyrighted reading passages.[1] In the mathematics review, staff of Harcourt-Brace Educational Measurement also expressed their desire to avoid "form bias," that is, the possibility that similar, but otherwise acceptable items might be grouped on the same form to a degree that would be unacceptable.

CONTENT REVIEWS

After the items were delivered to AIR from the subcontractors in reading or mathematics, they were reviewed individually for content, both by AIR staff and by external experts who are familiar with NAEP items.[2] In addition, a subset of almost 600 items was tried out in talk-aloud sessions with 4th- or 8th-grade students. As shown in Figure 3-1, all of these review processes took place simultaneously with item writing, between early April and late June 1998. According to the original plan, item revision and bias review would take place during the first week of July, and by mid-July AIR would begin to deliver items for final review by NAGB in three weekly batches of 850 to 900 each. NAGB would then have until its November meeting to review the item pool and approve a sufficient number as candidates for pilot testing. As described below, these plans were changed by NAGB in light of our interim report in July (National Research Council, 1998), which recommended changes in item review and revision schedules and processes.

Review and Revision Process

The item review and revision process includes a set of sequential and overlapping steps:

(1) initial review of items by the subcontractors for reading and mathematics development;
(2) content review by the prime contractor and its consultants;
(3) review by outside content experts;
(4) trial evaluation of a subset of items in one-on-one talk-aloud sessions with students (called cognitive labs);
(5) to the extent possible, provision of recommendations for item revision to item writers on the basis of summaries of information obtained from steps 1-4;
(6) review of items for bias and sensitivity by consultants to the contractors;
(7) revision of items by the item writers;

[1]The VNT specifications call for the use of published literary and informational passages, subject only to very minor editorial change with permission of the copyright holders.

[2]As noted above, all reading passages were reviewed by NAGB before any reading items were prepared.

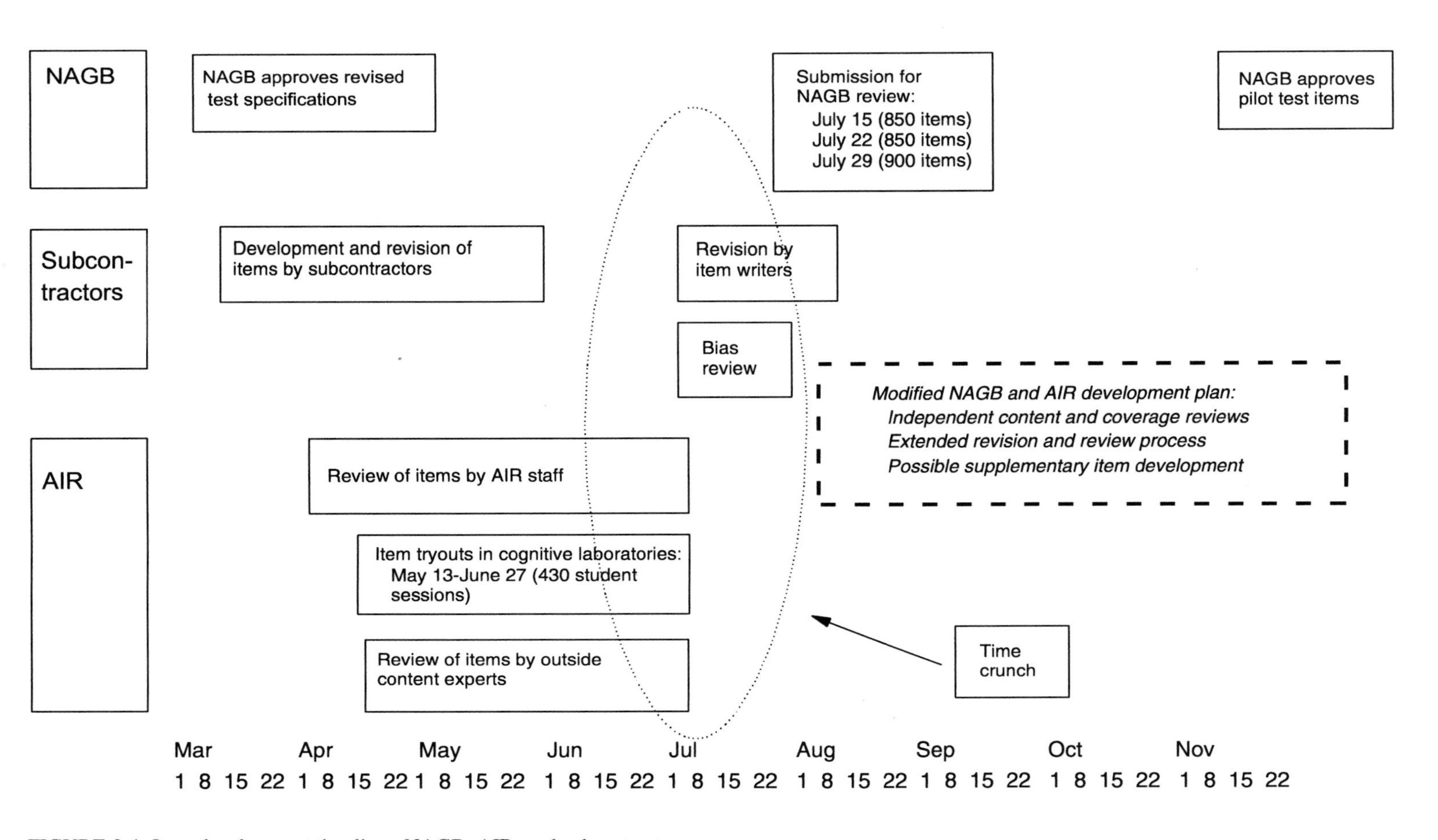

FIGURE 3-1 Item development timeline: NAGB, AIR, and subcontractors.

(8) review of test items by NAGB; and
(9) NAGB signoff on test items.

As shown in Figure 3-1, steps 1-5 above were to be completed by June 30, so that revisions to at least a subset of the approximately 2,600 items would be possible prior to the bias review that was scheduled for July 6-8. This bias review and the previously provided review information was to be the basis for additional item revision prior to NAGB's review and approval. NAGB was scheduled to review items in three waves, one beginning July 15, the next beginning on July 22, and the final beginning on July 29. Approval of the items would be sought at the November 1998 NAGB meeting. Approved items then would be assembled in draft test forms for the proposed pilot administration of the VNT in spring 1999. In this schedule, it was unclear what activities NAGB planned to undertake for its review between July 15 and the November meeting.

Assessment of Review and Revision Process: Interim Report

Our concern with the schedule resulted primarily from data obtained in our third workshop, on June 2-3, with a group of outside experts with experience in the development and evaluation of conventional and performance-based test materials (see Appendix C). The test developers supplied a list of items that represented the VNT specifications for content coverage and item formats. We selected a total of 60 mathematics items from a pool of 120 items provided by the prime contractor. Similarly, we selected 6 reading passages with a total of 45 items from a pool of 12 reading passages with roughly 90 questions. The sample of items we selected matched the VNT specifications for the length of a test form as well as for content coverage and item formats.

The experts examined and rated a subset of secure test items in their area of expertise.[3] Because the items we examined in June were products of the initial stages of item development, we did not expect them to reflect the complete development process. Many items had been through content review, and a number were being tried out with small numbers of students to assess item clarity and accuracy, but none of the items had been reviewed for bias or sensitivity, revised by test writers, or submitted for NAGB review and approval.

At the workshop, the experts independently identified the knowledge and skills likely to be measured by each item and attempted to match them to the content and skill outlines for the VNT. The experts also appraised item quality and identified ambiguities that might lead students to invalid responses (correct or incorrect). After the item rating exercise, the principal investigators and staff met jointly with the experts, NAGB, and the developers of the VNT to discuss issues of item quality and coverage and to discuss plans for item review and quality assurance. The principal investigators and staff also met separately with the experts for further discussion of the item materials.

On the basis of our evaluation of the information provided at the workshop, subsequent discussions, and the process and products of item development, we wrote an interim letter report in July (National Research Council, 1998). Although we benefited greatly from the views of the experts with whom we worked, we stress that the findings, conclusions, and recommendations were solely those of the authors and the NRC. We summarize that report here, but we stress that these findings apply only to the materials available to us by early June.

---

[3]Before examining the test materials, the experts, co-principal investigators, and NRC staff signed nondisclosure statements promising to protect the confidentiality of the materials. Consequently, specific illustrations of our findings cannot be provided without breaching the security of these materials.

The review plans for VNT items are appropriate and extend beyond procedures typically employed in test development. The plans for content review, student tryouts of items, and bias and sensitivity review appeared rigorous and thorough. The plans for student tryouts, in particular, went well beyond item review procedures found in most test development programs (see below, "Cognitive Laboratories"). These tryouts included extensive probes to determine the validity of the students' scored responses and to identify problems that may lead to correct answers when students do not have the targeted knowledge or skill or lead to incorrect answers when they do.

The draft items we examined were at an early stage of development, and many of them need improvement. We and our experts found items with ambiguities and other problems of construction. In the case of reading items, for example, there were items for which there was no clearly correct response, some with two possibly correct responses, and some with distracter options that might signal the correct answer. In addition, some items could possibly be answered without reading the associated passages, and others appeared to ask students to use supporting information for their response that was not in the text. Expert panelists flagged roughly one-half of the items available for our examination as requiring further review and possible revision.

It is critical to keep this finding in proper perspective. First, it is common to find problems with a significant number of items early in the item development process: Why conduct rigorous item reviews if not to weed out items that do not pass muster? The VNT developers, in fact, expected that 15 percent of the items would be eliminated from consideration even before pilot testing, and they also expected that only one-third or one-fourth of the piloted items would be used in the initial forms to be field tested for possible operational use. Moreover, as specific items were discussed at the workshop, the test developers who were present largely agreed with our assessment of item problems and in several cases reported that they had earlier come to the same conclusions.

Thus we conclude that there has not been sufficient time for the test development contractors to act on weaknesses in the test items. This conclusion about the unrefined state of the items we reviewed was by no means a final assessment of their quality. Rather, it signaled that a significant amount of review and revision would be required to achieve a final set of high-quality items. Furthermore we found:

- *The items examined did not appear to represent the full range of knowledge and skills targeted by the VNT content and skill outlines.* Although there were items that represented varied content areas and many of the less complex skill areas, few of the items in the sample were likely to assess higher-order thinking skills, as required by the approved test specifications. It will not be easy to revise items to cover these important parts of the skill specifications or the subareas of knowledge that might be underrepresented.
- *NAGB and its development contractor have also not yet had time to determine the extent to which the pool of items being developed will enable reporting of student performance in relation to NAEP's achievement levels, a central goal of VNT development.* As noted above, NAGB has developed specific descriptions of the skills associated with NAEP's basic, proficient, and advanced achievement levels for 4th-grade reading and 8th-grade mathematics (see the achievement-level descriptions in Appendix E). The validity of the achievement levels, which has been a topic of considerable discussion, depends on whether the description of each achievement level matches the skills of students classified at those levels (see Burstein et al., 1996; Linn, 1998; National Academy of Education, 1996; U.S. General Accounting Office, 1993). Comparing candidate VNT test items with the achievement-level descriptions is an important step to ensure coverage of each achievement level. In the items we and our experts reviewed, there appeared to be a shortage of items tapping higher-order skills. We urged NAGB

and its contractors to determine whether additional time and development were needed to produce enough items that test skills at the advanced achievement level.

- *The current schedule does not provide sufficient time for the provision of item review and tryout results to item authors and for the revision of item materials to ensure their accuracy, clarity, and quality.* Because of that schedule, a number of review activities that were more logically conducted in succession had been conducted simultaneously. These activities include content reviews by the prime contractor and its consultants, reviews by content experts, and the item tryouts. Furthermore, very little time was available to act on the results from each step in the review process: see the zone labeled "time crunch" in Figure 3-1. For the student tryout results to be of full use in further item development, reports on specific items had to be summarized and generalizations applied to the larger set of items not examined in the tryouts. Yet the schedule allowed less than 1 week between the conclusion of the cognitive sessions and the provision of feedback to the item writers. It also provided less than 1 week for revision of a large number of items prior to the bias and sensitivity review, planned for July 6, and only another week between the bias and sensitivity review and submission of the first wave of items to NAGB for its final review beginning July 15.

Given the large volume of items being developed, it appeared unlikely that any of these steps—summarizing review and tryout results, responding to bias and sensitivity reviews, and item revision—could be adequately completed, let alone checked, within the 1-week time frame scheduled for each of them. In other testing programs with which we are familiar, such as the Armed Services Vocational Aptitude Battery, the Medical College Admission Test, the Kentucky Instructional Results Information System, and the National Assessment of Educational Progress, this review and revision process takes several months.

These findings led to our central conclusion: **While the procedures planned for item review and revision are commendable, the current schedule for conducting review and revision appeared to allow insufficient time for the full benefit of those procedures to be realized.**

This conclusion led to our central recommendation: **We urge NAGB to consider adjusting the development schedule to permit greater quality control, and we suggest that it might be possible to do so without compromising the planned date for the administration of pilot tests (spring 1999).** Specifically:

- **We recommend that NAGB consider whether the remaining time for refinement of item materials by VNT developers and for item review and approval by NAGB should be reallocated to allow more time for the developers' careful analysis of item review information and for the application of this input to the entire set of items. The period of time allocated for NAGB's review of item materials might be reduced correspondingly, to allow for full and complete attention to item revision and quality assurance by the test development contractors.**

- **We recommend that NAGB and its contractors consider efforts now to match candidate VNT items to the NAEP achievement-level descriptions to ensure adequate accuracy in reporting VNT results on the NAEP achievement-level scale.**

- **We recommend that NAGB and its contractors consider conducting a second wave of item development and review to fill in areas of the content and skill outlines and achievement-level descriptions that appeared to be underrepresented in the current set of items.**

It is not yet possible to know the effect of our interim letter report and of NAGB's responses to it on the quality of the item pool for the VNT pilot test. However, NAGB's positive and constructive response to our recommendations leaves us cautiously optimistic about the outcome. As shown in Figure 3-1, NAGB modified the item development process, all consistent with its approval of the item pool by late November:

(1) NAGB extended the item development schedule by 3 months to permit more time for item development and review and to provide a greater opportunity for information from item reviews to be used in item revision and development. Final delivery of items by AIR to NAGB was moved from July 29 to October 30, 1998 (see Appendix F).

(2) AIR is adding two additional item review processes: independent content coverage reviews in mathematics and in reading and an independent review of the match between achievement levels and mathematics and reading items.

(3) NAGB's revised schedule includes time for another round of item development and review if that is necessary to fill gaps in item coverage.

COGNITIVE LABORATORIES

A total of 584 items—312 in mathematics and 272 in reading—were assessed in cognitive labs (see Table 3-6).[4] An attempt was made to include all of the extended constructed response items; however not all of the reading passages were approved in time for their associated constructed response items to be included. Between May 11 and July 2, 234 students participated in the reading lab sessions and 196 students participated in mathematics lab sessions. The use of cognitive labs in a project of this kind is an innovative and potentially significant tool for test item development. Information from the cognitive labs could improve item quality in two ways: by providing specific information about items that were tried out in the labs and by providing information that could be generalized and applied in the evaluation of items that were not tried out in the labs. Because of its potential importance, we observed and monitored the lab process from training through completion, and we subsequently observed a number of videotaped interviews and compared our assessments of items with those by AIR staff. (See Appendix G for the list of dates and sites at which training sessions and cognitive interviews were observed live or on videotape.)

The cognitive labs were spread out nationally across six sites: AIR offices in Palo Alto, California; Washington, D.C.; Concord, Massachusetts; newly developed sites in East Lansing, Michigan; San Antonio, Texas; and Raleigh, North Carolina.[5] Student participants in the labs were recruited through schools, churches, and youth organizations. The process was not random, but site coordinators monitored and controlled the demographic profile of participants in terms of race, ethnicity, gender, urban location, family income, and language use. Recruited students were of diverse social origins, but minority and Hispanic students, students from families of high socioeconomic status, and suburban and rural students were overrepresented. In addition, there were 23 students who are bilingual or for whom English is a second language, 11 in reading and 12 in math, who were provided translators as needed. In

[4]The items included 93 extended constructed response items, 289 short constructed response items, 49 gridded, 8 drawn, and 145 multiple choice items (American Institutes for Research, Cognitive Lab Report, July 29, 1998).

[5]The description of the cognitive labs is based on AIR's procedural report of July 29, 1998. Our observations about the labs and their findings follow that description.

TABLE 3-6 Distribution of Items Used in Cognitive Laboratories

Description	Number Developed as of 7/15/98	Number in Labs	Percent in Labs
Mathematics Items by Strand			
Number, properties, and operations	442	70	16
Measurement	319	56	18
Geometry and spatial sense	233	66	28
Data analysis, statistics, and probability	207	50	24
Algebra and functions	265	70	26
Total	1,466	312	21
Mathematics Items by Format			
Multiple choice	953	65	7
Gridded response	164	49	30
Drawn	20	8	40
Short constructed response	274	143	52
Extended constructed response	55	47	86
Total	1,466	312	21
Reading Items by Stance (Approach)			
Initial understanding	216	52	24
Developing an interpretation	971	82	8
Reader-text connect	158	60	38
Critical stance	399	78	20
Total	1,744	272	16
Reading Items by Format			
Multiple choice	1,300	80	6
Short constructed response	357	146	41
Extended constructed response	87	46	53
Total	1,744	272	16

reading, 32 students had special educational needs, and in mathematics 19 had special educational needs: the only accommodation provided for these students, however, was extra breaks during the 2-hour interview period.

Items were grouped in packets of about 14 mathematics items or 10 reading items. Each item was analyzed, and a written protocol, describing potential paths to correct or incorrect responses, was prepared as a guide for the interviewer. An effort was made to assess, before the actual interviews, what might be likely paths toward "hits" or "misses" that were "valid" or "invalid," that is, how a student might reach either a correct or incorrect answer for the right or wrong reasons. Some of the interviewers and protocol developers were novices and some were experienced cognitive interviewers. Some were knowledgeable about teaching and learning in the relevant grade levels and subjects, but others were not. All were trained and practiced intensively for this project. Each packet of items was assigned to two of the laboratory sites, yielding a total of no more than nine interviews per packet.

Cognitive interviews were videotaped to permit later staff review. After appropriate consent forms were signed, students were trained in the think-aloud protocol—attempting to verbalize their thoughts as they responded. For each item, the tryout was in two parts, a first phase "in which the interviewers used only general, neutral prompts while the students read through each question, thought aloud, and selected their answers," and a second phase, in which "the interviewers verified whether the students encountered any problems with the specific item, . . . the interviewers used more direct prompts and probes" (from AIR procedural report, p. 3). Students were encouraged to work through items at their own pace, and each packet was administered in the same order in each interview. Consequently, items that appeared toward the end of packets were sometimes skipped. Following the interview, a summary report on each item was to be prepared by the interviewer (on a "1-1 form"). AIR staff summarized findings from the nine tryouts of each item (on a "9-1-1 form"), entered the summaries in a database of potential items, and prepared feedback to item writers.

Our observations and monitoring of the training sessions, protocols, cognitive interviews, and item summaries show a mixed picture of operational and analytic achievement and of missed opportunity. Some of the problems are due, no doubt, to the compression of the item development schedule, both before and (as originally planned) after the completion of the laboratory sessions. We offer the following assessment of the cognitive labs:

(1) The promise of cognitive interviewing as a tool for item development is that it will add to the information obtained from standard content and bias review procedures before items are pilot or field tested. Because of the compressed time schedule, however, items were introduced into the cognitive lab sessions in relatively unrefined form, before the other review and revision processes had been completed. Thus, many of the item problems identified in the labs could easily have been identified at less cost in standard review processes, and there is no way to determine the extent to which the labs have actually improved item quality above and beyond the standard procedures.

(2) Training and interviewing for the cognitive labs began when operational procedures were still in development. Training materials were revised at each of three successive training sessions across the country (in Washington, D.C., Palo Alto, California, and East Lansing, Michigan), and retraining of interviewers and protocol writers was required. Procedures changed slightly in the course of the lab sessions, and some item protocols were never completed.

(3) Staff and interviewer experience with cognitive interview methods varied across sites. Staffs in Palo Alto, East Lansing, and Boston were most experienced, while those in Washington, San Antonio, and Raleigh were least experienced. There was some reassignment of protocols from one site to another, creating a heavy operational and quality control demand on sites that were initially most productive. This is reflected in AIR's list of the assignment of reading and mathematics protocols to sites, but the procedural report does not indicate the number of interviews contributed by each laboratory site.

(4) Just as interviewers varied in skill and experience, there was also variation in the quality of item protocols, despite substantial quality control efforts by AIR. This variation was a greater problem for inexperienced than for experienced interviewers, who did not rely as much on the protocols.

(5) Written item evaluations were sometimes prepared long after the interviews, rather than when interviewers' memories were fresh. For example, at the time our observers visited Palo Alto, their interviewers appeared to be 2 weeks behind in preparation of 1-1 forms, but those in East Lansing were only 2 days behind. This problem was theoretically mitigated by the availability of video recordings.

(6) The items in each packet were always presented to students in the same order. Not only did this yield more missing data from some items than others, but it also appears likely that there were fatigue and context effects on student responses to later items.

(7) The multisite plan for data collection is commendable because it yielded a diverse set of student subjects. At the same time, because of the developmental character of the process and the

uneven distribution of experience and skill across sites, there were operational problems in the coordination of activities and the workload distribution. However, in most cases, these problems were accommodated flexibly by redistribution of workload and of staff among sites.

(8) The original schedule for item development, review, and revision called for specific findings from the cognitive labs to be in the hands of the item-writing subcontractors for their use in revising items before the scheduled delivery of items to NAGB between July 15 and July 29. When the item reviews took place—at the end of the first week in July—the subcontractors had not yet received feedback from the cognitive labs.

(9) NRC staff members and consultants reviewed the videotapes of all 36 interviews conducted for a small set of items (seven items from two reading packets and five items from two mathematics packets). They then compared their own notes on each item—based on their reading of the item and its protocol as well as the cognitive interview—with the summary (9-1-1) form. There was general agreement with AIR's recommendations, but in several cases AIR appeared to be more optimistic about the potential of an item or less clear about directions for revising it than were our reviewers.

(10) There has as yet been no report by AIR about general lessons for item development or revision learned from the cognitive labs. In its procedural report of July 29, AIR states, "Assuming NAGB approval, an in-depth description of the cognitive lab data will appear in a subsequent report" (p. 4). We think that such a report could be useful in item review and revision during the current, extended development period.

The prima facie case for the value of cognitive interviews in item development remains strong. Direct evidence of students' understandings of language and items clarifies item content in ways that may not be apparent to adult experts. The cost-effectiveness issue is different: whether enough improvement was gained to warrant the expense is unknown and probably cannot be learned from these data. We think that it would be useful for AIR to attempt to draw general lessons from its experience in the current round of item development. Those data cannot, however, be useful in addressing the cost-benefit question because unrefined items were tested in the cognitive labs. Moreover, at this time there is inadequate evidence either of the specific or general contributions of the cognitive labs for VNT item review and revision. We think it is possible to produce and use such evidence in the item review and revision process before the November NAGB meeting, and we encourage NAGB to solicit this information before memories fade or the relevant AIR staff turn to other activities.

Given this year's experience, if the VNT project continues, we believe that AIR and its subcontractors should be well prepared to carry out and profit from cognitive laboratories of items during later rounds of item development. It should be possible to organize and schedule this activity to provide a cost-benefit analysis of standard item review and revision procedures in comparison with processes that include cognitive laboratories.

ONGOING REVIEW PROCESS

To assess progress in revising and editing VNT items, we visited AIR on July 28 and reviewed file information for a sample of reading and mathematics items. The sample, carefully selected to represent the entire domain of VNT items, consisted of three strata. The first stratum consisted of 30 of the mathematics items and 4 or 5 reading passages with about 20 associated items from the set of 105 items reviewed at the June 2-3 workshop. The second stratum consisted of 30 mathematics items and 4 reading passages with 20 associated items that were used in the four cognitive laboratory protocols that had previously been selected for intensive observation. The purpose of choosing these two strata was to allow us to examine progress in identifying and fixing specific item problems that we had identified earlier. The final stratum consisted of another 30 mathematics items and 20 reading items selected from items that had been added to the item bank after our June workshop.[6]

In all, we sought information on the status of 90 mathematics items and 60 reading items. For each sampled item, we recorded whether a folder was located; if so, the number of item reviews documented in the folder; the summary recommendation (accept, revise, drop) of each reviewer; whether reports from the cognitive laboratories were present; if so, whether changes were recommended to the item or to the scoring rubric (or both); and whether a final determination had been made to accept, drop, or revise the item.

Mathematics

File information was found for all but five of the items selected for our study: the missing five files were either in use by AIR staff or had been filed improperly and could not easily be located.

- Roughly 90 percent of the folders contained at least one review; 85 percent contained comments from more than one reviewer; 67 percent had three or more reviewers' comments.
- For 90 percent of the items at least one reviewer had recommended some revision. The percent of items that one or more reviewers recommended dropping was about 17 percent.
- Cognitive laboratory results were found for roughly two-thirds of the items that had been subjected to cognitive laboratories. Some of the information from the cognitive laboratories had not yet been put into the item folders, and some information may have been taken out for copying in response to a separate request we had made for information on laboratory results. When cognitive laboratory information was available, there were changes recommended to either the items or the scoring rubrics (or both) for 52 percent of the items.

Our best assessment of the position of these 90 mathematics items as of July 28 is that 13 percent would be accepted with no further changes, 57 percent would be accepted with minor revisions, 19 percent would be accepted with more significant revisions, and about 12 percent would be dropped. Overall, roughly 67 percent of the items that have been developed are required for the pilot test. For the items that we examined, the apparent retention rate (88 percent) was well above this level.

Reading

The reading files were kept by passage. Two of the passages that we selected had been dropped on the basis of bias reviewer comments or the cognitive laboratories. The file folder was not available for one other passage, and we obtained the folder for an additional passage used in our June workshop as a replacement. Reviewer comments were available for each of the passages we selected, and cognitive laboratory results were also available for each of the passages that had been included in one of the cognitive protocols. Most of the passages were still being worked on. It appears that about 30 percent of the sampled items would be accepted with no change, 49 percent would be accepted with revision,

[6]As noted above, the items selected for the June workshop constituted a representative sample of items available at that time.

and about 20 percent would be dropped. This number was also above the overall target of a 67 percent acceptance rate needed for the item requirements for the pilot test.

Summary

Overall, we recorded 24 specific comments made at our June workshop. Almost one-half of these concerns were also identified by the contractors' reviewers. Other comments may be picked up in subsequent reviews by contractor staff or by NAGB. Their reviewers also identified issues not raised at our expert workshop.

Our review of item files indicates a vigorous ongoing review and revision process. We believe that it confirms the concerns expressed in our interim letter report that the process could not have been successfully concluded by the end of July. As of the end of July, reviews had been completed on roughly one-third of the items in the pool, and it appears that the item drop rates will be less than the one-third anticipated in AIR's item development plans. Given that the majority of the items were still under review, this figure is rather tentative, and we cannot reach definitive conclusions about the quality or effect of the overall review process.

RECOMMENDATIONS

3-1. More time should be allowed for review and revision in future cycles of item development. To the extent possible, reviews should be conducted in sequence rather than in parallel so that the maximum benefit may be derived from each step in the review process.

3-2. The developers should improve and automate procedures for tracking items as they progress through the development cycle so as to provide timely warnings when additional items will be needed and historical information on item survival rates for use in planning future item development cycles. NAGB and the development contractor should monitor summary information on available items by content and format categories and by match to NAEP achievement-level descriptions to assure the availability of sufficient quantities of items in each category.

3-3. NAGB should undertake a careful study of the costs and benefits of the cognitive laboratories to determine their appropriate use in future development cycles.

4

VNT Pilot and Field Test Plans

After item development is completed, items will be assembled into tryout forms for pilot testing. The pilot test will provide empirical evidence on item quality that will be used in screening the Voluntary National Tests (VNT) items. Items that survive this screening will be assembled into six operational forms for the field test. Data on the statistical characteristics of these forms will be collected in the field test, providing the basis for equating the forms to each other (placing their scores on a common scale) and linking the scores from the forms to the National Assessment of Educational Progress (NAEP) scale and NAEP achievement levels. In addition, the field test will provide an important test of operational test administration procedures and provide a basis for linking VNT scores to the scale used to report 8th-grade mathematics results from the Third International Mathematics and Science Study (TIMSS).

PILOT TEST PLANS

Our second workshop, in April 1998, reviewed plans for conducting a pilot test of VNT items and plans for subsequent field test of VNT test forms (see Appendix B for the list of participants). Four documents from AIR were among the materials reviewed:

(1) Linking the Voluntary National Tests with NAEP and TIMSS: Design and Analysis Plans (February 20, 1998)
(2) Designs and Equating Plan for the 2000 Field Test (April 9, 1998)
(3) Designs and Item Calibration Plan for the 1999 Pilot Test (April 24, 1998)
(4) Sample Design Plan for the 1999 Pilot Test (April 28, 1998)

The quality of the VNT items selected for inclusion in operational forms and the accuracy with which those forms are pre-equated depend very heavily on the effectiveness of the pilot test plans. This chapter presents our findings and conclusions, based on the workshop review and our own review of subsequent documents.

Number of Items

Plans call for trying out 2,160 items, split evenly between 4th-grade reading and 8th-grade mathematics in the pilot test. For mathematics, a total of 360 items will be included in the six operational forms built for the field test. The number of mathematics items to be piloted, 1,080, is three times this number. Experience with similar programs (e.g., the Armed Services Vocational Aptitude Battery) suggests that, even with careful editing prior to the pilot test, as many as one-third of the items piloted may be flagged for revision or dropping based on item statistics from the pilot test (low item-total correlations, differential item functioning, out-of-range difficulties, positive item-total correlations for an incorrect option, high omit rates, etc.). The screening criteria for these decisions have not yet been specified. Many flagged items can be revised, but a subsequent pilot would be required to calibrate the revised items prior to selection for an operational form. However, even if the screening rate is twice as much (two-thirds) for some categories of items, the surviving one-third would be sufficient to construct six forms meeting the test specifications.

While the number of items piloted appears to be comfortably large, it does not appear to be inappropriately large. If the item survival rate is, indeed, two-thirds, there will be twice as many acceptable items as needed for the first set of operational forms. This number will allow items to be selected from each content and format category so as to create forms of similar difficulty, both overall and with equal difficulty in each content and format category. Remaining items can be held for use in future forms, so an overage would not waste effort. (Note that item development for subsequent forms should be targeted to fill in specific holes in the content, format, and difficulty distributions of the acceptable items not used in the first set of forms.)

For reading, the situation is a bit more complex because items are grouped in sets associated with particular passages. The survival rate of whole passages must be considered, along with the survival rate of individual items. Overall, 72 passages will be piloted, and one-half of this number will be needed to assemble six operational forms. Each passage will be piloted twice with separate item sets: for a passage to have enough items to be used operationally, an appropriately distributed 50 percent item survival rate will be required. The survival rate of multiple-choice items should not present a problem. Suppose a passage requires about 6 acceptable multiple-choice items of the 12 being tried out. If the survival rate is two-thirds (and failure probabilities are independent across items within a set), the probability of at least six items surviving is above 93 percent. For constructed-response items, the survival demands are a little higher. Many passages will require a single constructed-response item from two being developed for the pilot test. If the survival rate is two-thirds for each item, the chances of both items failing would be one-ninth, which is a passage survival rate of 89 percent. Under these assumptions, the chance of survival of both a sufficient number of multiple-choice and constructed-response items 0.93×0.89 or about 83 percent, well above the 50 percent survival rate required for a sufficient number of passages for the operational form.

We note, however, that there is no very good basis for estimating the survival rate for constructed-response items. Furthermore, the passage survival rate must be at least 50 percent for each of the five passage types (short, medium, and long literary passages and short and medium information passages). Even with the planned overage of passages, there is a significant possibility that an insufficient number of passages will survive screening rules in one or more of the passage type categories. Thus, it would be prudent to consider fallback options if this should occur. Such options might include relaxing the screening criteria (which have not yet been specifically stated) or allowing some modification of items or scoring rubrics between pilot and field tests. The latter option would reduce the precision with which forms are pre-equated with respect to difficulty and test information. This option could still be chosen if it is judged that the differences that do occur could be offset through equating adjustments.

Sample Size and Sampling Plan

The proposed plan calls for samples of 24,000 4th-grade students in 558 schools to participate in the pilot test of VNT reading items and 19,200 8th-grade students in 344 schools to participate in the pilot test of VNT mathematics items. The sample sizes were set to provide for response data from at least 800 students for each pilot test form. Two reading and two mathematics forms will each be administered to three such samples to permit linking across clusters of students, as described below. There will be a modest oversampling of schools with higher proportions of minority students so that approximately 150 Hispanic and 200 African American students will complete each test booklet.

While the current pilot test plan does not explicitly list the item statistics to be estimated for each item, common practice is to focus on the following: proportion passing (or proportion at each score level for items scored on a three- or five-point scale); item-total correlations; the frequency with which each distractor option is selected (for multiple-choice items); the proportion of examinees who do not respond to or do not reach an item; and differences in passing rates or mean scores for students from different demographic groups who are at the same level of overall ability (as estimated by the other items in the test). The demographic groups that are usually specified include females, African Americans, and Hispanics. In addition to these "conventional" statistics, item response theory (IRT) parameters will be estimated for each item for use in pre-equating alternative forms and for estimating test information functions that give the expected accuracy of a form at different score levels.[1]

A simple random sample of 800 students would lead to 95 percent confidence bounds for proportions of less than .035. Even allowing for a modest design effect due to the use of two-stage (geographic areas and then schools within sampled areas) rather than simple random sampling, the confidence bounds will still be less than .05. At this level of accuracy, there should be no problem in distinguishing relatively difficult items (passing proportions in the .3 to .4 range) from relatively easy items (passing proportions above .8). Similarly, with a sample size of 800, the standard error of a correlation would be about .035. This should be perfectly adequate for distinguishing items with acceptable item-total correlations (generally above .2 or .3) from items that do not correlate with what the rest of the test is measuring (generally, correlations that are zero or negative).

There are, of course, a very large number of items to be screened, requiring a large number of different statistical tests. Some items, near the cutoff for a screening decision, may be misclassified even with very large samples. Once a plan for specific screening decisions has been enunciated (e.g., eliminating items with unacceptable validity on differential item functioning [DIF] values), a more complete power analysis should be performed. The key point is that relatively small classification errors (e.g., accepting an item that is actually slightly below a cutoff) are not a major problem: normal item selection procedures avoid items that are near the boundary of a screening decision. Furthermore, since overall test difficulty and accuracy is related to averages of item statistics across all items in a test, small errors in statistics for individual items will tend to average out.

[1]Item response theory is a statistical model that calculates the probability each student will get a particular item correct as a function of underlying ability; for further discussion of IRT modeling, see Lord and Novick (1968).

The adequacy of the sample size for proposed analyses of DIF by demographic group is supported by prior research. For future revisions of this plan, however, we would welcome a more specific description of the size of differences that should be detected and the power of the proposed samples to detect those differences. Nonetheless, the proposed sample sizes for the targeted demographic groups are quite consistent with common practice, and we do not question them.

The chief focus of the analyses as described in the pilot test plan is "calibration" rather than screening. At the item level, calibration can mean simply estimating an item's difficulty. The more common meaning used here involves estimating parameters of item characteristic curves that predict the percent passing as a function of underlying ability level. The plan proposes using a computer program developed by the Educational Testing Service (ETS) called PARSCALE. This is the program that is used to produce item parameter estimates (and also student ability estimates) for NAEP. The plan does not go into detail on the estimation option(s) to be used with this program.

The uses of the item parameter estimates do not have major consequences. Estimates from the pilot test will not provide the basis for normative information to be reported to examinees, nor for the final equating of scores from alternative forms, each of which would be a significant use. Rather, item parameter estimates from the pilot test will be used to support construction of forms that are roughly equal in difficulty and accuracy so that form calibrations based on subsequent field test results will be feasible.

In the workshop review of the sampling plan, some concern was expressed about the possible underrepresentation of students from small rural schools and possibly also from private schools, where the number of students in the target grades was below the target for the number of students tested per school. (An average of about 42 4th-grade students would be tested from each school selected for the reading pilot and an average of about 56 8th-grade students would be tested from each school selected in the mathematics pilot.) We understand that this concern will be resolved or clarified in a subsequent revision of the sampling plan. In any event, this is a relatively minor concern for the pilot test, in which no attempt is being made to develop test norms or to equate alternative forms.

Plans for Pilot Test Form Design and Assignment

Pilot test plans call for the assembly of 18 distinct forms of mathematics items and 24 distinct forms of reading items. (We presume that each reading passage will be used in two different forms, with different sets of questions for each use.) The plan calls for the creation of a number of "hybrid" forms (22 in reading and 28 in mathematics) that consist of the first half (45-minute session) of one form paired with the second half of another form. Each form will resemble an operational form insofar as possible with respect to length and administration time, distribution of items by content and format, and distribution of items with respect to other factors (such as calculator use).

To reduce risks associated with compromise of test security, the number of different items administered in any one school will be limited to one-third of the total set of pilot test items. Schools will be divided into four clusters. Two forms will be administered in all four clusters to provide a basis for linking the performance scales developed for each cluster of schools and forms. The remaining forms will be assigned to only one of the four school clusters. Hybrid forms will be similarly assigned to specific clusters of schools. Within each school in a specific school cluster, a total of six intact and six hybrid mathematics or eight intact and eight hybrid reading forms will be distributed to students in a spiraled fashion. Spiralling is an approach to form distribution in which one copy of each different form, from first to last, is handed out before "spiralling down" to a second copy of each form and then a third and so forth. The goals of this approach are to achieve essentially random assignment of students to forms while ensuring that an essentially equal number of students complete each form.

The current design involves a wide range of assumptions about time requirements, student endurance, and other aspects of test administration. The pilot test affords an opportunity to test some of these assumptions at the same time that data for item screening and calibration are collected. In addition, trying out items in forms that differ from their operational use (in length or content context) may introduce additional sources of error in parameter estimates.

An earlier version of the pilot test plan included an option for schools to participate on a more limited basis, with each student taking only half of a complete form (e.g., only one 45-minute testing session). We hope that this option is no longer being considered, as it would create several problems. For example, the proposed DIF analyses require sorting students into groups by overall level of performance and comparing the passing rates within groups. We question the accuracy with which students who take only half a form would be assigned to these groups. But, if students who take only half a test are excluded from the DIF analyses, the sample sizes might not be adequate to support such analyses. These issues would have to be addressed if the "half-test" option is reconsidered.

The plan for limiting item exposure to specific clusters of schools introduces significant complexity into the pilot test design. Such complexity appears warranted because, even if the likelihood of test item compromise is not high, the consequences would be very large. It would be useful to know what other measures are planned to ensure test security. Will each booklet have a unique litho code so that missing booklets can be identified and tracked down? How will each test session be monitored? How will materials be shipped and stored?

The stated reason for having hybrid forms is to explore "susceptibility to context effects" and reduce "the impact of locally dependent items in the pilot test calibration" (American Institutes for Research, Designs and Item Calibration Plan for the 1999 Pilot Test, July 24, 1998). Since each half-form (45-minute testing session) remains intact, the potential for introducing context effects or local item dependence appears minimal. In reading, the plan is for a particular passage type to always appear within the same session and in the same position. In this case, item position effects are not an issue. For mathematics, item positions are not fixed, so items used in one position in the pilot test could be used in a quite different position in an operational form. A more effective design for addressing this issue would be to create alternate versions of each mathematics form with the same items presented in reverse order.

We believe that the reason for using hybrid forms, while not explicitly stated, is to improve the degree to which parameter estimates for items appearing in different forms can be put on the same scale. If hybrid forms are not used, there is no overlap across forms: the only way to link the parameter estimates for different forms within a given school cluster is through the assumption that random assignment of forms to students eliminates the need for further adjustment. Item calibrations would be performed separately for each form, setting the underlying performance scale to have a mean of 0 and a standard deviation of 1 (or any other desired constants). For random samples of 800, the sampling error for mean performance would be about .035 standard deviations. With spiraling, however, a (nearly) equal number of students take each form within each school, eliminating between-school differences in sampling error. Consequently, the standard error of differences between the performance means of the samples of students taking different forms would be much less than .035. This level of error seems modest and perfectly adequate, given the intended uses of the pilot test item parameter estimates, particularly in light of other sources of variation (e.g., context effects, differences in student motivation). Under the hybrid form design, only 400 students would complete each distinct form. A key question is whether the error in adjustments to put the 400 student samples on a common scale would not be greater than the sampling error that this approach seeks to reduce.

Differences between school clusters might be more significant. The use of an anchor form to identify differences in the performance distribution of students from different school clusters appears prudent. The use of two anchor forms, as suggested by the contractor's Technical Advisory Committee and reflected in the revised plan, appears even more prudent. It would still be reasonable, however, to expect a more explicit discussion of the level of error that could be encountered without such an anchoring plan and the degree to which the use of anchors will reduce this error. Each cluster includes from 86 to 149 different schools; with the careful assignment of schools to clusters, the potential for significant differences in student performance across clusters does not appear to be great.

The use of hybrid forms will introduce a number of problems that are not specifically addressed in the current plans. In conducting DIF analyses, for example, it might be problematic to use an observed total score (with or without the item in question removed) as the basis for conditioning on overall performance. Because students taking hybrid forms take the first half of one test form and the second half of another, it is not possible to calculate total scores for use in analyzing differential item functioning. This form assignment model effectively splits student sample sizes in half and reduces the power to detect significant differences in item functioning. Presumably, students would be sorted on the basis of item-response-theory ability estimates (theta) rather than observed scores. The weighting of item types could vary from one form to another, and the estimation of performance may be poor for some students with discrepant response patterns. A demonstration of the approach to be used would be appropriate. The use of hybrid forms also significantly increases the complexity of form distribution within a school. If only intact forms are used, either six or eight different forms would have to be distributed to the (up to) 50 students participating from the school. With hybrid forms, the number of different forms to be distributed would increase to 12 to 16. Random assignment of students to forms will work because differences in student performance average out over a large number of students. When there are more forms, there are fewer students per form and thus a somewhat greater degree of sampling error.

Summary and Conclusions

Given the goal of assembling six operational forms from the pilot test item pool and current plans for review and revision of items prior to the pilot test, we find the number of items to be piloted to be appropriate, reflecting relatively conservative assumptions about item survival rates.

The proposed sample size and sampling plan is fully acceptable for meeting the objectives of the pilot test.

We believe the sample size to be adequate, even in the absence of some detail on the approach to estimating item parameters.

We strongly endorse the plan to create pilot forms that resemble operational forms to the maximum extent possible.

We also endorse the plan to limit item exposure within any one school.

We are not convinced that the complexity of the design for hybrid forms is justified by potential gains in statistical accuracy.

Overall, we believe the plans for pilot testing VNT items to be generally sound. The number of items to be piloted and the proposed sample sizes appear entirely appropriate to the goals of creating six operational forms that meet test specifications and are adequately pre-equated. We have raised several questions about details of the design and the plans for analyzing the resulting data. The issues raised are mostly details and do not affect the recruiting of schools, which must begin soon. We believe there is sufficient time for revisions and clarifications to the plan and consideration of any proposed changes by the National Assessment Governing Board (NAGB) at its November 1998 meeting. Any remaining issues could be resolved with ample time to proceed with implementation of the pilot test as planned in March 1999.

Recommendations

4-1. Back-up options should be planned in case the survival rates of items in the pilot test are lower than currently estimated.

If pilot test results lead to elimination of a larger than expected number of items, NAGB will have to consider back-up options for constructing and field testing test forms. Alternatives might include: reducing the number of new test forms to be included in the first operational administration; relaxing the item screening criteria to allow greater use of statistically marginal items; finding additional sources of items (e.g., NAEP or commercial item pools); and delaying the field test until further items can be developed and screened. Although we believe that such options are not likely to be needed, planning for unanticipated outcomes is prudent.

4-2. Prior to any large-scale data collection, the discussion of analysis plans for the pilot test should be expanded to provide a more explicit discussion of: (a) the item-level statistics to be estimated from the pilot test data, (b) decision rules for screening out items based on these statistics, (c) how the statistics on surviving items will be used in assembling operational forms, and (d) the rationale for the level of accuracy that will be achieved through the proposed data collection design.

4-3. The plans for hybrid test forms should be dropped, or the rationale for using them should be specified in much more detail and be subject to review by a broad panel of psychometric experts. On the basis of our understanding of the hybrid forms, we recommend not using them.

4-4. The procedure that will be used to assign items to pilot test forms should be described in more detail.

Questions such as the following should be addressed. Will assignment be random within content and format categories or will there be attempts to balance pilot forms with respect to other factors (e.g., the issue of potential "form bias" identified in the subcontractors' item bias reviews)? What sort of review will be conducted to identify potential problems with duplication or cueing (the text of one item giving away the answer to another)?

FIELD TEST PLANS

Our review of the field test plans is, necessarily, less extensive than our review of plans for the pilot test. The plans developed to date are preliminary; the current contract schedule calls for revised field test plans to be developed by the contractor and reviewed by NAGB toward the end of fiscal 1999 (September 30). Furthermore, the determinations that NAGB must make about item quality will be based on pilot test data. The field test is designed to collect and evaluate information about whole test forms; further decisions about individual items will not be made on the basis of data from the field test.

Our review of the field test plans is based on the documents provided by NAGB and AIR for review at our April workshop:

Designs and Equating Plan for the 2000 Field Test, April 9, 1998
Linking the Voluntary National Tests with NAEP and TIMSS: Design and Analysis Plans, February 20, 1998

We have not received or reviewed any subsequent versions nor are any scheduled for development and review until summer 1999.

The field test plans that we reviewed were similar in content to the pilot test plans. They describe the number of forms that will be fielded, the size of the sample of schools and students to whom each form will be administered, and, in broad terms, the analyses to be performed.

Forms

Plans call for six forms (designated A through F) of each test to be included in the field test. Four forms would be targeted for operational use—an operational form for each of the next 3 years and an anchor form to be used in all 3 years for equating purposes. In addition a "research form" would be developed for use in future research studies, including checks on the stability of linkage over time. A sample form would also be field tested and equated and then given out in advance of the first operational testing to provide users with an example of an intact form.

The plan calls for the first two forms—the Year 1 form (A) and the equating form (B)—to be treated differently from the other forms. They will be administered to larger samples of students (see below) in a separate equating cluster.

No reason is given why the Year 1 operational form needs greater precision in equating than the Year 2 and Year 3 operational forms. Plans for the use of the anchor form (B) are sketchy at best and do not include adequate rationale.

Plans also call for field testing hybrid versions of the operational forms. These would be combinations of the first half (testing session) of one form and the second half of a different form. The use of hybrid forms assumes that apropriate IRT scoring methods will be used to calculate scores from which the achievement-level classifications will be made (with estimates derived using IRT pattern matching).[2] The hybrid form approach attempts to maximize accuracy in calculating individual item statistics by controlling for differences in the samples of students receiving different forms. The primary purpose of the field test, however, is to examine test score statistics, not item statistics. NAGB and its contractor have not yet publicly decided whether IRT pattern scoring or observed total correct scores should be used as the basis for achievement-level classifications.

Sample Size

The current field test plan calls for sample sizes of 1,000 for each intact and 1,000 for each hybrid version of the research and public release forms and the forms targeted for operational use in Years 2 and 3. Considerably larger samples would be used for the Year 1 and anchor forms. For the reading

[2] With IRT pattern scoring, the credit a student receives for a particular correct response depends on the examinee's pattern of responses to other related items (see Lord and Novick, 1968).

forms, 4,500 students would complete each of the intact and hybrid versions, and twice as many students would complete the mathematics forms.

The proposed sample sizes for equating alternative operational forms are consistent with common practice. Samples of 2,500 test takers per form are used to develop an initial equating of new forms of the Armed Services Vocational Aptitude Battery (ASVAB), for instance. The ASVAB is a relatively high-stakes test, used to qualify applicants for enlistment, so the initial equating is subsequently verified by a re-equating, based on operational samples of about 10,000 applicants per form.

There are two rationales for the larger sample sizes proposed for Forms A and B. First, they may be used to collect normative information, even though plans for norm-based reporting have neither been proposed nor approved. It seems likely that NAGB will want to use data from NAEP as a basis for providing much more extensive normative information. It is also possible that normative information could be constructed from the data collected for all six forms if forms are adequately equated.

The other rationale for large sample sizes for Forms A and B is that they will be used separately to develop the linkage to NAEP achievement levels. The even larger sample sizes proposed for mathematics may be based on the desire to link mathematics scores to the TIMSS scale, as well as to NAEP. It is not clear why this linkage needs to be based on two forms and not either one or all of the forms, presuming an adequate equating of forms.

Equating Cluster Design

The current plan calls for the use of three separate equating clusters so that no more than half of the forms are administered in any one school. The need for test security is incontrovertible. Indeed, it is so strong that the plans for administering the tests must ensure that not even one form is compromised at any location. So long as such procedures are in place, the added complexity of the equating cluster design may be unnecessary. A far simpler design would be to randomly (through "spiraling") assign students within each school to the six forms.

Analysis Plans

Preliminary analysis plans were developed by the contractor and presented to NAGB's design and methodology subcommittee at its March 1998 meeting. These plans, which were also reviewed in our April 1998 workshop, are necessarily preliminary. As noted in Chapter 6, decisions about scoring and scaling procedures have not been made. The draft equating plan describes procedures for putting item parameters on a common scale. This approach is consistent with the use of IRT scoring. If NAGB adopts a simpler approach on the basis of total scores, item calibration will not be needed as a step in equating.

Preliminary plans for linking VNT scores to NAEP and TIMSS are generally consistent with recommendations of the Committee on Equivalency and Test Linkage (National Research Council, 1999c). Plans call for administration of each of the measures to be linked under conditions that are as identical to operational use as possible. Students will take the NAEP assessment in February, the VNT in March, and TIMSS in April, using the administrative procedures associated with each of these assessments. Attempts will be made to account separately for sampling, measurement, and model misspecification errors in assessing the overall accuracy of each linkage. Differences in the linkages across different demographic groups will be analyzed. The initial proposal also includes efforts to monitor stability over time.

In other chapters of this report, we note that accuracy targets have not been set in advance in specifying test length or form assembly procedures. Similarly, current plans do not include targets for equating and linking accuracy. The accuracy with which students are assigned to achievement levels will depend directly and perhaps heavily on equating and linking accuracy, so further accuracy goals are needed.

Summary and Conclusions

The field test plans that we reviewed lacked sufficient rationales for several elements of the proposed design, including the use of hybrid forms, the use of equating clusters, and differential sample sizes for different forms. A key problem in creating greater specificity is that plans for scoring the operational forms have yet to be discussed. In addition, accuracy targets for reporting—and hence for equating—also do not yet exist.

We find insufficient justification for the disparate treatment of the Year 1 (A) and equating (B) forms and the other forms (C-F).

The hybrid forms design is totally incompatible with the use of total correct scores and may not even be a very good idea if IRT pattern scoring is to be used.

Recommendations

4-5. Plans for VNT scoring should be developed, reviewed, and approved prior to completion of revised field test plans.

Scoring plans should specify whether total correct or IRT pattern scoring will be used and should indicate accuracy targets that would provide a basis for determining the accuracy with which alternative forms must be equated.

4-6. Only intact forms (i.e., not hybrid forms) should be used.

Whether or not IRT scoring is adopted, the rationale for the use of hybrid forms is weak at best.

4-7. Unless a much stronger rationale is presented, the goal should be to equate all forms with the same accuracy, and plans for different sample sizes for different forms should be changed.

4-8. Analyses should be conducted to demonstrate the level of accuracy of equating results for targeted sample sizes. NAGB should review and approve equating accuracy targets prior to adoption of the final field test plans.

4-9. The final field test plans should include an evaluation of the need for separate equating clusters. Unless a strong need for the separate clusters is demonstrated, the sample design should be simplified.

5

Inclusion and Accommodation

In the November 1997 legislation that established the National Assessment Governing Board's (NAGB) responsibility for the development of the Voluntary National Tests (VNT), Congress required NAGB to make four determinations. The third of these is "whether the test development process and test items take into account the needs of disadvantaged, limited English proficient and disabled students" (P.L. 105-78: Sec. 307 (b) (3)). The same legislation called on the National Research Council (NRC) "to evaluate whether the test items address the needs of disadvantaged, limited English proficient, and disabled students."

There are two key challenges to testing students with disabilities or limited English proficiency. The first challenge is to establish effective procedures for identifying and screening such students, so they can appropriately be included in assessment programs. Federal law and state and local policy increasingly demand participation of these special populations in all education activities, both as a means of establishing the educational needs and progress of individual students and for purposes of system accountability. The second challenge is to identify and provide necessary accommodations (e.g., large-print type, extended time) to students with special needs while maintaining comparable validity of test performance with that in the general population (see National Research Council, 1997, 1999b). That is, any accommodation should alter only the conditions of assessment without otherwise affecting the measurement of performance. This issue is growing in importance, along with the number of students with disabilities or with limited English proficiency. Students with disabilities now comprise 12.3 percent of all students in elementary and secondary school, and students with limited English proficiency are 5.5 percent of all students.

FINDINGS

While NAGB has just approved a set of "principles" for the inclusion and accommodation of students with disabilities and limited English proficiency in the pilot test of the VNT (National Assessment Governing Board, 1998c), there has as yet been little developmental work on the project to address the special needs of these populations. The 430 participants in cognitive laboratory sessions included students with disabilities (32 in reading and 19 in math) and limited English proficiency (11 in reading and 12 in math), but their numbers were too small to provide substantial or reliable information about the participation of such students in the VNT.

In addition to the statement of principles, the American Institutes for Research (AIR) has two planning documents: "Revised Inclusion and Accommodations Work Plan" (May 8, 1998), which was approved by NAGB at its May meeting, and "Background Paper Reviewing Laws and Regulations, Current Practice, and Research Relevant to Inclusion and Accommodations for Students with Disabilities" (July 23, 1998). AIR has also developed lists of organizations with particular interest in the educational and testing needs of students with disabilities or limited English proficiency for NAGB's use in holding public hearings about inclusion and accommodation. We understand that a parallel background paper on inclusion and accommodation of students with limited English proficiency will be presented to NAGB at its November 1998 meeting. As noted above, we know of no VNT development activities or plans specifically aimed at the needs of disadvantaged students or those with limited English proficiency, but such students did participate in one development activity—the cognitive labs.

Because of the compressed schedule in the early phases of VNT development, along with the desire to achieve close correspondence between the VNT and NAEP, the NAGB plans and the AIR background paper on students with disabilities both focus on recent NAEP practices for inclusion and accommodation, rather than taking a broader, more proactive stance. We believe the federal government has an important leadership role to play in subsidizing and demonstrating valid efforts to include these populations.

The procedures discussed in the draft documents are intended to increase participation and provide valid assessments for all students, but they essentially involve retrofitting established assessment instruments and procedures to special populations of students; another approach would be to design and develop assessments from the beginning that are accessible to and valid for all students.

From its beginning around 1970 and through the middle 1990s, NAEP assessments were carried out without accommodation of any kind. Procedures for "inclusion" usually focused on the exclusion of some students from the assessments, rather than on universal participation. Since the mid-1990s, as the growth of special student populations and the importance of their participation in large-scale assessments have increasingly been recognized, NAEP has experimented with new, more inclusive participation and accommodation policies, which are recapitulated with reference to the VNT in the NAGB principles and AIR planning documents. For example, in NAGB's draft principles, and depending on the test and population in question, accommodations for the pilot test may include large-print booklets, extended time, small-group administration, one-on-one administration, a scribe or computer to record answers, reading a test aloud by an examiner, other format or equipment modifications, or a bilingual dictionary if it is normally allowed by the school. However, the success of these policies in increasing participation is not yet established, nor have their effects on test performance and score comparability been validated.

Unless extensive development work is done with students with disabilities and with limited English proficiency, it would be unreasonable to expect that the VNT will be valid for use with these student populations. Both of these populations are heterogeneous, e.g., in primary language, level of proficiency in English, and specific type of disability. Moreover, they differ from the majority of students, not only in ways that affect test-taking directly—e.g., those that can be accommodated through additional time or assistive devices—but also in styles of learning and in levels of motivation or anxiety. Such differences are very likely to reduce the validity and comparability of test performance.

The Committee on Appropriate Test Use has identified two important ways in which inclusion and accommodation can be improved (National Research Council, 1999b). First, the focus should be on inclusion and accommodation issues throughout item and test development, so a test is designed from the ground up to be accessible and comparable among special populations. For example, the NRC report recommends oversampling of students with disabilities and with limited English proficiency in the course of pilot testing so there will be sufficient numbers of cases in major subgroups of these students to permit DIF analyses. Second, test developers should explore the use of new technologies, such as computer-based, adaptive testing for students who need extra time, which show promise of substantially reducing or eliminating irrelevant performance differentials between many students who require accommodation and other students. The NRC Committee on Appropriate Test Use recognized, however, that development work of this kind is just beginning, and there are presently few successful exemplars of it.

CONCLUSION

The statement of principles and the AIR planning documents provide a limited basis for evaluation of provisions for inclusion and accommodation in the VNT—and no specific basis to address the quality of item development relative to the needs of those students.

NAGB's desire to maintain correspondence between NAEP and the VNT has not precluded departure from current NAEP practices in other areas—for example, the use of intertextual items and gridded responses. In our judgment, a major opportunity for improved large-scale assessment is being lost in NAGB's conservative approach to inclusion and accommodation in the VNT.

RECOMMENDATION

5-1. NAGB should accelerate its plans and schedule for inclusion and accommodation of students with disabilities and limited English proficiency in order to increase the participation of both those student populations and to increase the comparability of VNT performance among student populations.

This recommendation requires prompt action because so much of the development work in the first round of the VNT has already been completed. We have already noted the modest attention to students with special needs in the cognitive laboratory sessions. In the pilot test, NAGB plans to identify students with disabilities and with limited English proficiency and with the types of accommodations that have been provided. However, there are no provisions in the design to ensure that there will be sufficient numbers of these students—such as students requiring specific types of accommodation—to support reliable DIF analyses. We think that it would be feasible to include larger numbers of such students in the pilot and field tests, for example, by increasing sampling fractions of such students within schools. Moreover, there appears to be no plan to translate the 8th-grade mathematics test into Spanish (or any other language), a decision that is likely to affect participation in the VNT by major school districts. There has been some discussion of a Spanish translation after the field test, but this would be too late for the item analyses needed to construct comparable English and Spanish forms.

6

Reporting

The National Assessment Governing Board (NAGB) has made very clear its intention that Voluntary National Tests (VNT) results should be reported using National Assessment of Educational Progress (NAEP) achievement levels. Presumably, this means that each student and his or her parents and teachers would be told whether performance on the test reflects below basic, basic, proficient, or advanced mastery of the reading or mathematics skills outlined in the test frameworks.

More specific discussion of reporting has been largely postponed. NAGB reviewed a "Revised Test Result Reporting Work Plan (American Institutes for Research [AIR], April 23, 1998) at its May 1998 meeting. This plan outlined a number of research steps, from literature review through focus groups, that might be undertaken to identify and resolve reporting issues and problems. The plan did not propose any specific policies or even attempt to enunciate key reporting issues. The schedule called for approval of field test reporting plans by NAGB in August 1999, with decisions on reporting for the operational test in August 2000. In this section, we discuss four key issues in reporting VNT results and describe implications of decisions about these issues for other test development activities.

KEY ISSUES

The charge for phase 1 of our evaluation does not emphasize evaluation of reporting plans and, as indicated above, final decisions on many reporting issues are not yet available for review. Nonetheless, several reporting issues are discussed here that we hope will be addressed in the final plans for reporting. These include:

- the validity of the achievement-level descriptions,
- communicating uncertainty in VNT results,
- computing aggregate results for schools, districts, and states, and
- providing more complete information on student achievement.

The Validity of the Achievement-Level Descriptions

NAEP's procedures for setting achievement levels and their results have been the focus of considerable review (see Linn et al., 1991; Stufflebeam et al., 1991; U.S. General Accounting Office, 1993; National Academy of Education, 1992, 1993a, 1993b, 1996; National Research Council, 1999a). Collectively, these reviews agree that achievement-level results do not appear to be reasonable relative to numerous other external comparisons, such as course-taking patterns and data from other assessments, on which larger proportions of students perform at high levels. Furthermore, neither the descriptions of expected student competencies nor the exemplar items appear appropriate for describing actual student performance at the achievement levels defined by the cutscores. Evaluators have repeatedly concluded that the knowledge and skills assessed by exemplar items do not match up well with the knowledge and skill expectations put forth in the achievement-level descriptions, nor do the exemplars provide a reasonable view of the range of types of performance expected at a given achievement level.

The design of the VNT will expose the achievement-level descriptions to a much higher level of scrutiny than has previously occurred. They will be applied to individual students—not just to plausible values. The classification of students into the achievement levels will be based on a smaller set of items than is used in a NAEP assessment, and all of these items will be released and available for public review. Judgments about the validity of the achievement level descriptions will be based in large part on the degree to which the items used to classify students into achievement levels appropriately match the knowledge and skills covered in the achievement-level descriptions.

In Chapter 2 we recommend greater integration of the achievement-level descriptions with the test specifications, and in Chapter 3 we recommend matching the VNT items to the knowledge and skills in these descriptions. Consideration should also be given to ways in which the link between items and the achievement-level descriptions could be made evident in reporting. For example, the description of proficient performance in 4th-grade reading includes "recognizing an author's intent or purpose," while the description of advanced performance includes "explaining an author's intent, using supporting material from the story/informational text." Given these descriptions, it would be helpful to provide information to students classified at the proficient level as to how they failed to meet the higher standard of advanced performance.

Communicating Uncertainty in VNT Results

Test results are based on responses to a sample of items provided by the student on a particular day. The statistical concept of reliability focuses on how much results would vary over different samples of items or at different times. In reporting aggregate results for schools, states, or the nation, measurement errors are averaged across a large number of students and are not a critical factor in the accuracy of the results. When results are reported for individual students, however, as they will be for the VNT, measurement error is a much more significant issue.

The report of the Committee on Equivalency and Linkage (National Research Council, 1999c) describes how the same student could take several parallel versions of the VNT and end up with different, perhaps even quite different, achievement-level classifications. Such possibilities raise two key issues for reporting:

- How can uncertainty about test scores best be communicated to parents, teachers, and other recipients of test results?
- How much uncertainty will users be willing and able to tolerate?

Computing Aggregate Results for Schools, Districts, and States

Another issue identified by the Committee on Equivalency and Linkage concerns differences in reporting individual and aggregate results. NAEP uses sophisticated methodology to provide accurate estimates of the proportion of students at each achievement level. These methods involve conditioning on background variables and creating multiple "plausible values" for each student on the basis of their responses to test questions and their background information. (For a more complete explanation of this methodology, see Allen et al., 1998.)

We believe that student-level reporting will drive the need for accuracy in VNT results, but tolerance for different levels of accuracy in aggregate results should be explored before final decisions about test accuracy requirements are reached. The VNT contractors have begun to discuss alternatives for reporting aggregate results, ranging from somewhat complex procedures for aggregating probabilities of being at each level for each student through ways of distancing results from the two programs so that conflicts will not be alarming and, perhaps, not even visible.

One way of resolving the aggregation issue that has not been extensively discussed would be to generate two scores for each student. The first, called a reporting score, would be the best estimate of each students' performance, calculated either from a tally of correct responses or using an IRT scoring model. The second, called an aggregation score, would be appropriate for estimating aggregate distributions and would be based on the plausible values methodology used for NAEP (see Allen et al., 1998, for a discussion of the plausible values method).

Providing More Complete Information on Student Achievement

A key question that parents and teachers are likely to have is how close a student is to the next higher (or lower) achievement-level boundary. This question is particularly important for the presumably large proportion of students whose performance will be classified as below the basic level of achievement.

Diagnostic information, indicating areas within the test frameworks for which students had or had not achieved targeted levels of proficiency, could serve very useful instructional purposes, pointing to specific areas of knowledge and skill in which students are deficient. The amount of testing time required for providing more detailed information accurately is likely to be prohibitive, however. In addition, the fact that the NAEP and VNT frameworks are designed to be independent of any specific curriculum further limits the instructional value of results from the VNT.

Using subcategories or a more continuous scale (such as the NAEP scale) for reporting nearness to an achievement boundary may be much more feasible given current test plans for length and accuracy levels. It might be possible, for example, to report whether students are at the high or low end (or in the middle) of the achievement level in which they are classified. Using such a scale, however, would require acceptance of an even greater level of uncertainty than would be needed for the achievement-level reporting.

CONCLUSIONS

Our key conclusion with regard to reporting is that a clear vision of how results will be reported should drive, rather than follow, other test development activities. If NAEP achievement-level descriptions are used in reporting, the map of test items to specific elements of these descriptions should be made evident. Decisions that affect factors that influence the accuracy of VNT results will also have to be made well in advance of the dates proposed for NAGB approval of reporting plans. As described above, decisions about test length, a key determinant of test score accuracy, have already been made without careful consideration of the level of accuracy that can be obtained with the specified test length. Other factors, such as item calibration and equating and linking errors, also influence the accuracy of VNT test results.

Methods used by NAEP, including conditioning and plausible values, are not appropriate for reporting individual student results and are not needed for VNT. Without some adjustments, however, VNT results for individual students, when aggregated up to the state level will disagree, in some cases markedly, with NAEP estimates of student proficiency, so that the credibility of both programs will be jeopardized. This will occur even if there are no differences in the levels of student motivation for the VNT and NAEP.

No decision has been made about whether and how results will be reported in addition to the achievement levels. It seems likely that students, particularly those in the below basic category, will benefit from additional information, as will their parents and teachers.

RECOMMENDATIONS

6-1. NAGB should accelerate its discussion of reporting issues, with specific consideration of the relationship between test items and achievement-level descriptions.

Rather than waiting until August 1999, it would be prudent for NAGB and its contractors to determine how achievement-level information will be reported and examine whether items are sufficiently linked to the descriptions of the achievement levels. In addition, attention is needed to the level of accuracy likely to be achieved by the VNT as currently designed and to ways of communicating the corresponding degree of certainty to potential test users.

6-2. NAGB should develop ways of communicating information to users about measurement error and other sources of variation in test results.

6-3. NAGB should develop and review procedures for aggregating student test results prior to approving the field test reporting plan.

6-4. NAGB and AIR should develop and try out alternative ways of providing supplemental test result information. Policies on reporting beyond achievement-level categories should be set prior to the field test in 2000, with a particular focus on students who are below the basic level of achievement.

References

Allen, Nancy L., James E. Carlson, and Christine A. Zelenak

1998 *The 1996 NAEP Technical Report*. Washington, DC: U.S. Department of Education.

Applebome, Peter

1997 U.S. is seeking more influence over education. *New York Times* August 31:A1.

Burstein, L., D. Koretz, R. Linn, B. Sugrue, J. Novak, E.L. Baker, and E.L. Harris

1996 Describing performance standards: Validity of the 1992 National Assessment of Educational Progress achievement-level descriptors as characterizations of mathematics performance. *Educational Assessment* 3(1):9-51.

Council of Chief State School Officers and MPR Associates, Inc.

1997a Item and Test Specifications for the Voluntary National Test in 8th Grade Mathematics. Recommendations to the National Test Panel. Mathematics Subcommittee, Test Specifications Committee, Council of Chief State School Officers, and MPR Associates, Inc., Washington DC.

1997b Item and Test Specifications for the Voluntary National Test in 4th Grade Reading. Recommendations to the National Test Panel. Reading Subcommittee, Test Specifications Committee, Council of Chief State School Officers, and MPR Associates, Inc., Washington DC.

Linn, Robert L.

1998 Validating inferences from National Assessment of Educational Progress achievement-level setting. *Applied Measurement in Education* 11(1):23-47.

Linn, Robert L., Daniel M. Koretz, Eva L. Baker, and Leigh Burstein

1991 *The Validity and Credibility of the Achievement Levels for the National Assessment of Educational Progress in Mathematics*. Los Angeles, CA: Center for the Study of Evaluation, University of California.

Lord, Frederic M., and Melvin R. Novick

1968 *Statistical Theories of Mental Test Scores*. Reading, MA: Addison-Wesley.

National Academy of Education

1992 *Assessing Student Achievement in the States*. Robert Glaser, Robert Linn, and George Bohrnstedt, eds. Panel on the Evaluation of the NAEP Trial Assessment. Stanford, CA: National Academy of Education.

1993a *Setting Performance Standards for Student Achievement*. Robert Glaser, Robert Linn, and George Bohrnstedt, eds. Panel on the Evaluation of the NAEP Trial Assessment. Stanford, CA: National Academy of Education.

1993b *The Trial State Assessment: Prospects and Realities*. Robert Glaser, Robert Linn, and George Bohrnstedt, eds. Panel on the Evaluation of the NAEP Trial Assessment. Stanford, CA: National Academy of Education.

1996 *Quality and Utility: The 1994 Trial State Assessment in Reading.* Robert Glaser, Robert Linn, and George Bohrnstedt, eds. Panel on the Evaluation of the NAEP Trial State Assessment. Stanford, CA: National Academy of Education.

National Assessment Governing Board

1998a Test Specifications Outline: Voluntary National Test in 8th Grade Mathematics. Adopted March 7. National Assessment Governing Board, Washington, DC. Available electronically at http://www.nagb.org

1998b Test Specifications Outline: Voluntary National Test in 4th Grade Reading. Adopted March 7. National Assessment Governing Board, Washington, DC. Available electronically at http://www.nagb.org

1998c Voluntary National Tests: Inclusions and Accommodations for Test Development. Policy statement, draft, July 7. National Assessment Governing Board, Washington, DC.

no date a *Mathematics Frameworks for the National Assessment of Educational Progress: 1992-98.* Washington, DC: National Assessment Governing Board.

no date b *Reading Frameworks for the National Assessment of Educational Progress: 1992-98.* Washington, DC: National Assessment Governing Board.

National Research Council

1997 *Educating One and All: Students with Disabilities and Standards-Based Reform.* Lorraine M. McDonnell, Margaret J. McLaughlin, and Patricia Morison, eds. Committee on Goals 2000 and the Inclusion of Students with Disabilities, Board on Testing and Assessment, National Research Council. Washington, DC: National Academy Press.

1998 Letter to Secretary Richard Riley, U.S. Department of Education, and Mark D. Musick, National Assessment Governing Board, from Robert Hauser and Lauress Wise, co-principal investigators, on Evaluation of the Voluntary National Tests. Board on Testing and Assessment, National Research Council, Washington, DC, July 16.

1999a *Grading the Nation's Report Card: Evaluating NAEP and Transforming the Assessment of Educational Progress.* James W. Pellegrino, Lee R. Jones, and Karen J. Mitchell, eds. Committee on the Evaluation of National and State Assessments of Education, Board on Testing and Assessment, National Research Council. Washington, DC: National Academy Press.

1999b *High Stakes: Testing for Tracking, Promotion, and Graduation.* Jay P. Heubert and Robert B. Hauser, eds. Committee on Appropriate Test Use, Board on Testing and Assessment, National Research Council. Washington, DC: National Academy Press.

1999c *Uncommon Measures: Equivalence and Linkage Among Educational Tests.* Michael J. Feuer, Paul W. Holland, Bert F. Green, Meryl W. Bertenthal, and F. Cadelle Hemphill, eds. Committee on Equivalency and Linkage of Educational Tests, Board on Testing and Assessment, National Research Council. Washington, DC: National Academy Press.

Resnick, Lauren

1987 *Education and Learning to Think.* Committee on Mathematics, Science, and Technology Education, Commission on Behavioral and Social Sciences and Education, National Research Council. Washington, DC: National Academy Press.

Riley, Richard

1997 Letter to the editor. *Washington Post* August 30:A26.

Stufflebeam, Daniel L., Richard M. Jaeger, and Michael Scriven

1991 Summative Evaluation of the National Assessment Governing Board's Inaugural 1990-1991 Effort to Set Achievement Levels on the National Assessment of Educational Progress. Prepared for the National Assessment Governing Board, August 23.

U.S. General Accounting Office

1993 *Educational Achievement Standards: NAGB's Approach Yields Misleading Interpretations.* GAO/PEMD-93-12. Washington, DC: U.S. General Accounting Office.

1998 *Student Testing: Issues Related to Voluntary National Mathematics and Reading Tests.* GAO/HEHS-98-163, June. Washington, DC: U.S. General Accounting Office.

Appendices

APPENDIX

A

Workshop on Item and Test Specifications for VNT

DECEMBER 5-6, 1997

Panelists and Invited Participants

Joan Auchter, GED Testing Service
Stephen Dunbar, University of Iowa
Jeremy Finn, Temple University
Bert Green, John Hopkins University
John Guthrie, University of Maryland
Andy Hartman, The National Institute for Literacy
Bill Honig, San Francisco State University
Eugene Johnson, Boston College
Sylvia Johnson, Howard University
Patricia Kenney, Learning Research and Development Center, University of Pittsburgh
Jeremy Kilpatrick, University of Georgia
Stephen Klein, RAND
Mary Lindquist, Columbia State University
Peter Pashley, Law School Admission Council
Jack Stenner, Metametrics
David Thissen, Chapel Hill, North Carolina

Other Participants

Donald Burdick, Metametrics
Mary Crovo, National Assessment Governing Board
Richard Durán, University of California, Santa Barbara (BOTA)
Christopher Edley, Jr., Harvard Law School (BOTA)
Steve Ferrara, American Institutes for Research
Ray Fields, National Assessment Governing Board

Tom Fisher, National Assessment Governing Board
Adina Kole, U.S. Department of Education
Mark Kutner, American Institutes for Research
Archie LaPointe, American Institutes for Research
Sharon Lewis, Council of the Great City Schools
Robert Linn, University of Colorado (BOTA)
David Mandel, MPR Associates
Wayne Martin, Council of Chief State School Officers
John Olson, American Institutes for Research
Audrey Pendleton, U.S. Department of Education
Gary Phillips, U.S. Department of Education
Terry Salinger, American Institutes for Research
Sharif Shakrani, National Assessment Governing Board
Catherine Snow, Harvard University (BOTA)
Larry Snowhite, McA Enterprises
Holly Spurlock, U.S. Department of Education
Richard Stombres, Staff of Representative William Goodling
Kent Talbert, Staff of Representative William Goodling
William Taylor, Attorney at Law, Washington, D.C. (BOTA)
William Trent, University of Illinois, Urbana-Champaign (BOTA)
Roy Truby, National Assessment Governing Board
Jennifer Vranek, ACHIEVE
Kenneth Wolpin, University of Pennsylvania (BOTA)

APPENDIX B

Workshop to Review VNT Pilot and Field Test Plans

APRIL 30, 1998

Panelists

Lizanne DeStefano (via phone), Bureau of Educational Research, University of Illinois, Urbana-Champaign
Brad Hanson, American College Testing, Iowa City, IA
Benjamin King, National Opinion Research Center, Boca Raton, FL
Michael Kolen, Iowa Testing Programs, University of Iowa
Margaret McLaughlin, Institute for the Study of Exceptional Children, University of Maryland
Alan Nicewander, Defense Manpower Data Center, Seaside, CA
Linda Wightman, Department of Educational Research Methodology, University of North Carolina, Greensboro

Other Participants

Sue Betka, U.S. Department of Education
Mary Lyn Bourque, National Assessment Governing Board
Joseph Conaty, U.S. Department of Education
Mary Crovo, National Assessment Governing Board
Lawrence Feinberg, National Assessment Governing Board
Steven Ferrara, Center for Education Assessment
Raymond Fields, National Assessment Governing Board
William Morrill, MathTech
John Olson, American Institutes for Research
Audrey Pendleton, U.S. Department of Education
Gary Phillips, U.S. Department of Education
Keith Rust, Westat
Sharif Shakrani, National Assessment Governing Board
Fran Stancavage, American Institutes for Research
David Stevenson, U.S. Department of Education
Roy Truby, National Assessment Governing Board

APPENDIX
C
Workshop on VNT Item Development

JUNE 2-3, 1998

Panelists

Peter Afflerbach, Curriculum and Instruction, University of Maryland
Lizanne DeStefano, Bureau of Educational Research, University of Illinois, Urbana-Champaign
Roberta Flexer, Department of Education, University of Colorado
John Guthrie, Department of Human Development, University of Maryland
Patricia Kenney, Learning Research and Development Center, University of Pittsburgh
Marjorie Lipson, Department of Education, University of Vermont
William Tate, School of Education, University of Wisconsin-Madison

Other Participants

Rebecca Adamson, Mathtech, Inc., Princeton
Carol Benjamin, National Assessment Governing Board
Clayton Best, American Institutes for Research
Mary Lyn Bourque, National Assessment Governing Board
Mary Crovo, National Assessment Governing Board
Larry Feinberg, National Assessment Governing Board
Ray Fields, National Assessment Governing Board
Mark Kutner, American Institutes for Research
Archie LaPointe, American Institutes for Research
Diane Leipzig, National Assessment Governing Board
William Morrill, Mathtech, Inc., Princeton
John Olson, American Institutes for Research
Audrey Pendleton, U.S. Department of Education
Elizabeth Rowe, American Institutes for Research

Terry Salinger, American Institutes for Research
Sharif Shakrani, National Assessment Governing Board
Gary Skaggs, National Assessment Governing Board
Roy Truby, National Assessment Governing Board
Don Wise, Mathtech, Inc., Princeton

APPENDIX D

Source Documents

The following documents were provided by the American Institutes for Research:

Background Paper Reviewing Laws and Regulations, Current Practice, and Research Relevant to Inclusion and Accommodations for Students with Disabilities. July, 23, 1998.
Cognitive Lab Report. July 29, 1998.
Designs and Equating Plan for the 2000 Field Test. April 9, 1998.
Designs and Item Calibration Plan for the 1999 Pilot Test. April 24, 1998.
Designs and Item Calibration Plan for the 1999 Pilot Test. July 24, 1998.
Linking the Voluntary National Tests with NAEP and TIMSS: Design and Analysis Plans. February 20, 1998.
Proposed Plan for Calculator Use. July 23, 1998.
Proposed Plan for Determining Equivalency of Readability of NAEP and VNT Passages. July 23, 1998.
Proposed Year 2 Research Plan. July 23, 1998.
Report on Scoring Rubric Development. July 23, 1998.
Revised Inclusion and Accommodations Work Plan. May 8, 1998.
Revised Test Result Reporting Work Plan. April 23, 1998.
Revised Test Utilization Guidelines Work Plan. April 24, 1998.
Sample Design Plan for the 1999 Pilot Test. April 28, 1998.
Validity Research Agenda Work Plan. April 24, 1998.

The following additional documents were provided to us:

Harcourt-Brace Educational Measurement, Training Materials for the Voluntary National Test in Mathematics. Undated.
National Assessment Governing Board, Voluntary National Test: Inclusions and Accommodations for Test Development, Policy Statement, Draft. July 7, 1998.
Riverside Publishers, Directions to Item Writers for the Voluntary National Test in Reading. Undated.

APPENDIX E
Descriptions of Achievement Levels for Basic, Proficient, and Advanced

READING: 4TH GRADERS

Basic Level (208)

Fourth-grade students performing at the basic level should demonstrate an understanding of the overall meaning of what they read. When reading text appropriate for 4th graders, they should be able to make relatively obvious connections between the text and their own experiences.

For example, when reading literary text, basic-level 4th-grade students should be able to tell what the story is generally about—providing details to support their understanding—and be able to connect aspects of the stories to their own experiences.

When reading informational text, basic-level 4th graders should be able to tell what the selection is generally about or identify the purpose for reading it; provide details to support their understanding; and connect ideas from the text to their background knowledge and experiences.

Proficient Level (238)

Fourth-grade students performing at the proficient level should be able to demonstrate an overall understanding of the text, providing inferential as well as literal information. When reading text appropriate to fourth grade, they should be able to extend the ideas in the text by making inferences, drawing conclusions, and making connections to their own experience. The connection between the text and what the student infers should be clear.

For example, when reading literary text, proficient-level 4th graders should be able to summarize the story, draw conclusions about the characters or plot, and recognize relationships such as cause and effect.

When reading informational text, proficient-level 4th-grade students should be able to summarize the information and identify the author's intent or purpose. They should be able to draw reasonable conclusions from the text, recognize relationships as cause and effect or similarities and differences, and identify the meaning of the selection's key concepts.

Advanced Level (268) Fourth-grade students performing at the advanced level should be able to generalize about topics in the reading selection and demonstrate an awareness of how authors compose and use literary devices. When reading text appropriate to 4th grade, they should be able to judge texts critically and, in general, give thorough answers that indicate careful thought.

For example, when reading literary text, advanced-level 4th-grade students should be able to make generalizations about the point of the story and extend its meaning by integrating personal experiences and other readings with the ideas suggested by the text. They should be able to identify literary devices such a figurative language.

When reading informational text, advanced-level 4th graders should be able to explain the author's intent by using supporting material from the text. They should be able to make critical judgments of the form and content of the text and explain their judgments clearly.

MATHEMATICS: 8TH GRADERS

Basic Level (262) Eighth-grade students performing at the basic level should exhibit evidence of conceptual and procedural understanding in the five NAEP content strands. This level of performance signifies an understanding of arithmetic operations—including estimation—on whole numbers decimals, fractions, and percents.

Eighth graders performing at the basic level should complete problems correctly with the help of structural prompts such as diagrams, charts, and graphs. They should be able to solve problems in all NAEP content strands through the appropriate selection and use of strategies and technological tools — including calculators, computers, and geometric shapes. Students at this level also should be able to use fundamental algebraic and informal geometric concepts in problem solving. As they approach the proficient level, students at the basic level should be able to determine which of the available data are necessary and sufficient for correct solutions and use them in problem solving. However, these 8th graders show limited skill in communicating mathematically.

Proficient Level (299) Eighth-grade students performing at the proficient level should apply mathematical concepts and procedures consistently to complex problems in the five NAEP content strands.

Eighth graders performing at the proficient level should be able to conjecture, defend their ideas, and give supporting examples. They should understand the connections between fractions, percents, decimals, and other mathematical topics such as algebra and functions. Students at this level are expected to have a thorough understanding of basic-level arithmetic operations—an understanding sufficient for problem solving in practical situations. Quantity and spatial relationships in problem solving and reasoning should be familiar to them, and they should be able to convey underlying reasoning skills beyond the level of arithmetic. They should be able to compare and contract mathematical ideas and generate their own examples. Those students should make inferences from data and graphs; apply properties of informal geometry; and accurately use the tools of technology. Students at this level should understand the process of gathering and organizing data and be able to calculate, evaluate, and communicate results within the domain of statistics and probability.

Advanced Level (333) Eighth-grade students performing at the advanced level should be able to reach beyond the recognition, identification, and application of mathematical rules in order to generalize and synthesize concepts and principles in the five NAEP content strands.

Eighth graders performing at the advanced level should be able to probe examples and counterexamples in order to shape generalizations from which they can develop models. Eighth graders performing at the advanced level should use number sense and geometric awareness to consider the reasonableness of an answer. They are expected to use abstract thinking to create unique problem-solving techniques and explain the reasoning processes underlying their conclusions.

APPENDIX F
Revised Item Development and Review Schedule for VNT

Below is a summary of the key dates in 1998 for delivery of items, NAGB review, and panel meetings:

Date	Activity
8/18-25	Achievement level review panels
8/18-22	Content expert panels
9/1-4 (tent.)	Content coverage panels
9/28	1st batch of math items to NAGB
10/5	1st batch of reading items to NAGB
10/16	Reviews back from NAGB
10/30	Final batches of items to NAGB
11/13	Final reviews back from NAGB
11/19-21	NAGB final action on items

The following chart summarizes the review panels, tentative meeting dates, purpose, and composition:

Review Panel	Tentative Dates	Purpose	Composition
Ongoing Reading Expert Panel (ORE)	8/18-8/20	To review items, using information from cognitive labs, with the goal of providing final recommendations to the publishers	Content experts, including teachers and curriculum specialists with experience in elementary school reading instruction
Ongoing Math Expert Panel (OME)	8/20-8/22		Teachers and curriculum specialists with experience in middle school math instruction
Independent Reading Achievement Levels Panel (IRAL) and Independent Math Achievement Levels Panel (IMAL)	Early September	To ensure that the NAEP achievement levels are well covered by the VNT items	Teachers, curriculum experts and teacher educators familiar with NAEP achievement levels and content areas of math and reading
Independent Reading Content Coverage Panel (IRCC) and Independent Math Content Coverage Panel (IMCC)	First week of September	To ensure that the NAEP content frameworks are well covered by the VNT items	Teachers, curriculum experts, and teacher educators familiar with NAEP content frameworks

The following table summarizes the revised plans for VNT item development:

Month	Date	Activity
July	7/27-28	• Readability study held at AIR
	7/27-31	• Identify ORE and ON-IE Panel members • Plan expanded item review activities, including budget • Identify ORE and OME Panel members • Arrange for meeting space • Determine review sequence for items (e.g., ECRs first in math, intertextual sets first in reading)
	Late July	• SAC #1 reviews reading items via teleconference
August	8/3-7	• Receive all reading and math items in their most current state from publishers • Contact IRAL, IMAL, IRCC, and IMCC Panel members

Month	Date	Activity
		• Prepare items and related cognitive lab data in preparation for OME and ORE Panel meetings
		• Develop OME and ORE Panel meeting agendas
		• Design format/process for providing recommendations to publishers from OME and ORE Panel meetings
		• Begin reviewing cognitive lab tapes for rubric development and to inform content panels
	8/5-6	• SAC # 2 reviews math items in person
	8/6-8	• NAGB meeting
	8/10-14	• Finish preparing meeting materials for OME and ORE Panels
		• Begin preparing materials for IRAL and IMAL Panel meetings
		• Begin preparing student work for rubric refinement
	8/10	• Rubric refinement work begins at Harcourt and Riverside
	8/18-21 (tentative)	• IRAL Panel meeting
	8/22-25 (tentative)	• IMAL Panel meeting
	8/18-20 (tentative)	• OME Panel meeting
	8/20-22 (tentative)	• ORE Panel meeting
	8/24-9/4	• Process reviews from OME and ORE Panels
		• Send revision requests to publishers as completed
		• Send final recommendations to Harcourt and Riverside by 9/4
September	First week of September	• IRAL and IMAL Panel meetings
	Mid-September	• Additional OME and ORE Panel meetings, as needed
		• Revisions to math and reading items processed at AIR
		• Requests for revision sent to Harcourt and Riverside
	9/21	• First batch of revised items due from Harcourt and Riverside
	9/21-10/2	• Check revised items to prepare for NAGB
		• Prepare items for submission to NAGB
	9/28	• Math items submitted to NAGB
	September - October	• Additional item development, if needed, based on IRAL, IMAL, IRCC, and IMCC Panel meetings
October	10/5	• Reading items to NAGB
	October	• Continue process of reviewing OME and ORE experts' comments on reading and math items
		• Submit requests for revision to publishers
		• Process items as they are returned from publishers
	10/16	• All reviews to items in batch #1 returned from NAGB.
	10/30	• Final batch of math and reading items to NAGB for review (assuming no new item development)

Month	Date	Activity
November	11/2	• AIR completes review of newly developed items, if necessary
	11/3-10	• Publishers revise newly developed items, if necessary
	11/16	• Newly developed items to NAGB for review, if necessary
	11/13	• Final NAGB review of items (excluding any newly developed items)
	11/19-21	• NAGB Board meeting and final action on items • Final NAGB review of newly developed items
	11/30	• NAGB Reading and Math Committees final action on newly developed items, if necessary
December	December	• Pilot test forms assembled
January	1/1/1999	• Camera-ready copy to printers

APPENDIX

G

Observations of Cognitive Labs and Bias Reviews

Activity	Observations	Purpose of Observation
Cognitive Lab Training Palo Alto, CA (May 11-12, 1998) East Lansing, MI (April 20-21, 1998)	Participated in training provided to cognitive lab interviewers. Training consisted of two days of overview, tape observation, role playing, and discussion.	To acquaint evaluators with the interview methodology used in the cognitive labs. Also, attending both sessions provided evaluators with the ability to observe the evolution of the training materials.
Live Cognitive Lab Interviews AIR, New England (May 26, 1998) San Antonio, TX (June 8-9, 1998) AIR, Palo Alto (June 10-12, 1998) East Lansing, MI (June 22-23, 1998)	M2 (2 taped) R9 (1 taped) R7 (1 live interview, 1 taped) R16 (2 live interviews) R4 (4 taped) R9 (4 taped) M7 (1 live interview, 4 taped) M10 (2 live interviews, 1 taped) R20 (1 live, 1 taped) M11 (1 live interview) M19 (1 live interview) M16 (live interviews) R22 (1 taped) R18 (1 taped) R22 (1 taped)	To allow evaluators to observe the cognitive lab process and to determine whether the cognitive labs would provide information that could improve the quality of items. Observing interviews at several locations allowed evaluators to determine interviewer quality and whether the interviews were being conducted consistently across sites.

Activity	Observations	Purpose of Observation
Taped Cognitive Lab Interviews		
AIR, Washington, D.C. (July 1-2, 1998)	M2, M10 (9 tapes [some of which had already been seen] and 1-on-1 forms) R4, R9 (9 tapes [some of which had already been seen] and 1-on-1 forms)	To allow evaluators to focus on the contribution of the cognitive labs to item quality for a small sample of items and to allow evaluators to review the 1-on-1 forms filled out by the AIR interviewers.
Bias and Sensitivity Review		
Math—San Antonio, TX (July 6-7, 1998)	Panel members reviewed 1,400-1,500 items.	To determine the impact of bias and sensitivity review on item quality.
Reading—Chicago, IL (July 6-7, 1998)	Panel members reviewed 350-400 passages.	

APPENDIX

H

Biographical Sketches

Robert M. Hauser is the Vilas Research and Samuel A. Stouffer professor of sociology at the University of Wisconsin-Madison. His current research includes the Wisconsin Longitudinal Study, data from which are used for studies of aging and life course and social stratification, and the Study of Trends in the Schooling of Black Americans, an effort to trace trends in school enrollment, aspirations, and attainment of black Americans from the 1940s to the 1980s. He is a member of the National Academy of Sciences. Dr. Hauser received a B.A. degree in economics from the University of Chicago and M.A. and Ph.D. degrees in sociology from the University of Michigan.

Lauress L. Wise is president of the Human Resources Research Organization (HumRRO) in Alexandria, Virginia. His research interests focus on issues related to testing and test use policy. He recently served on the National Academy of Education's Panel for the Evaluation of the National Assessment of Educational Progress (NAEP) Trial State Assessment and is currently serving on the National Research Council's Committee on the Evaluation of NAEP. Prior to joining HumRRO, he directed research and development of the Armed Services Vocational Aptitude Battery (ASVAB) for the U.S. Department of Defense. In that capacity, he oversaw a study investigating the feasibility of linking ASVAB and NAEP mathematics scores. Dr. Wise received a Ph.D. degree in mathematical psychology from the University of California, Berkeley.

Stephen E. Baldwin is a senior program officer with the Board on Testing and Assessment. He has worked on labor, training, and education issues as an economist for the federal government and as a consultant, and he has taught at several universities. He holds B.A., M.A. and Ph.D. degrees, all in economics, from the University of Washington, Seattle.

Marilyn Dabady has served as a research associate for the Board on Testing and Assessment during the past two summers. She is a Ph.D. candidate in psychology at Yale University, where her research examines diversity in teams, race and gender discrimination, and intergroup relations. Ms. Dabady holds a B.A. degree from the State University of New York at Albany and an M.S. degree from Yale University, both in psychology.

Michael J. Feuer is director of the Board on Testing and Assessment. His past positions include senior analyst and project director, U.S. Office of Technology Assessment, where he directed studies on testing and assessment, vocational education, and educational technology, and assistant professor, Department of Management and Organizational Sciences, at Drexel University. His major areas of interest include human resources, education, and public policy. He has published numerous articles in scholarly journals as well as in the popular press. Dr. Feuer received a B.A. degree from Queens College, City University of New York, and M.A. and Ph.D. degrees from the University of Pennsylvania.

Viola C. Horek is administrative associate of the Board on Testing and Assessment. Before joining the board, she worked at the Board on Agriculture and the Committee on Education Finance of the National Research Council. Previously, she worked for the city of Stuttgart, Germany, as an urban planner and for the U.S. Department of Defense in Germany. Ms. Horek received an M.A. degree in architecture and urban planning from the University of Stuttgart.

Dorothy R. Majewski is a senior project assistant with the Board on Testing and Assessment. Prior to joining the staff of the Board on Testing and Assessment, Ms. Majewski worked in the Division of Health Promotion and Disease Prevention of the Institute of Medicine. Ms. Majewski received a B.A. degree in education from Carlow College in Pittsburgh, Pennsylvania.

Karen J. Mitchell is a senior program officer with the Board on Testing and Assessment. Previously, she was at RAND, where she conducted research on student assessment, education reform, and education policy. Dr. Mitchell has a B.A. degree in early childhood and elementary education from Wesleyan College and M.S. and Ph.D. degrees in educational research methodology from Cornell University.